NOT FOR THE FAINT OF HEART

T. L. BLAYLOCK

WESTBOW®
PRESS
A DIVISION OF THOMAS NELSON
& ZONDERVAN

WestBow Press books may be ordered through booksellers or by contacting:

WestBow Press
A Division of Thomas Nelson & Zondervan
1663 Liberty Drive
Bloomington, IN 47403
www.westbowpress.com
1 (866) 928-1240

ISBN: 978-1-4908-2038-5 (sc)
ISBN: 978-1-4908-2039-2 (hc)
ISBN: 978-1-4908-2037-8 (e)

Library of Congress Control Number: 2013923048

Printed in the United States of America.

WestBow Press rev. date: 01/07/2014

I dedicate this book to all those

I have failed as a husband,

as a father, as a brother

and as a friend.

What is man that You magnify him,

and that You are concerned about him,

that you examine him every morning

and try him every moment?

(Job 7:17-18)

Contents

1

Introduction

What is it that keeps you going day after day? What pulls on the strings of your heart? What do you long for in your dreams, working hard day after day to make it a part of your life? What drives you and fills your deepest longing? Have you found it yet or does it seem to be elusive, unattainable? Is there someone or something keeping you from finding it? Is your life filled with things to do or jobs that need to be done? Are you working day in and day out, trying to fulfill your deepest desires?

Maybe your life is filled with things you believed would satisfy that yearning, but they just leave you empty and longing for more. In every person, there is this innate desire calling out to be fulfilled; and yet, whatever it is, you cannot seem to put your finger on it. It is elusive, evasive, just beyond your reach — yet there, day after day, with the desire to be fulfilled. Maybe it has been right next to you, within reach; and all you have to do is to call out in order to begin enjoying a life filled with adventure and great possibilities.

I want you to know that "it" has been pursuing you relentlessly, even longing for you, hoping for you, loving you in a way that you have never been loved. It has been calling your name, orchestrating situations and circumstances in your life, trying to get you to understand that it is what your heart desires. You have been chasing the wind and grasping at nothing — working, seeking, striving. All the things you have acquired and all the relationships you have built have left you frustrated. You are unhappy, without purpose or direction, and still searching for something to fill that void. Many live life unfulfilled and empty as this longing continues to gnaw; but you have run out of energy. Your want-to seems to have subsided and you are too tired to fight anymore, too tired to go on, since it all seems hopeless. But there is hope.

Even if you consider yourself an atheist, I want you to know that God believes in you and will not give up trying to bring you closer to Him. I know many believe that Christianity is a crutch; but, without a doubt, we all have crutches. Yours may be pride, thinking you are a self made whatever — you fill in the blank. The truth is that God has helped you succeed regardless of your beliefs. Maybe your crutch is alcohol, pornography, sex, drugs (illegal or over-the-counter). Are you pouring your life into computer games or sports or work? Or do you spend your life in front of the television or computer screen, vicariously living life through your favorite movie star, sports fan, or newscaster? You know what or who you lean on, what you depend on to get you through each day — the only problem is that you are left empty, never satisfied, and without any real purpose or direction for life.

If you will continue reading, I will point you right to the doorstep of hope. I will prove to you what will fulfill your deepest desires and all of your longings — because that thing your heart has been yearning for is literally standing right beside you. "It" is God! Give me a chance and I will show you that the innate desire within each one of us can only be fulfilled by God Himself — our Creator, the One who made the heavens and the earth (including you) and sustains everything in them. What do you have to lose? Just read a few more pages. Then, if you are not satisfied, throw this book aside, continue down the path you are on, living a life that leaves you heartbroken, empty, unfulfilled, and always wanting more.

2

Living by Faith

God's greatest desire is for you to believe that He exists. Stop for a moment, examine your life, and try to see that God has allowed good and bad things to happen to draw you near to Him. God has been silently working behind the scenes to show you that He is the only one who is able to give your life meaning, direction, and hope. But, for the most part, you have kept God at arm's length through unbelief. The Bible says that "without faith it is impossible to please Him, for he who comes to God must believe that He is and that He is a rewarder of those who seek Him" (Hebrews 11:6). In order to have faith in God, you have to believe in Him and put your trust in Him. You do this by building a relationship with the one true God.

I have a friend who would say, "How can I believe in something I don't believe in?" My answer is that each one of us must choose to believe. Once you have chosen to believe in God, He will fill your heart with joy, peace, and hope. If you continue to read, you will come to know that God is real and that He has been trying to reveal Himself to you your whole life. But first things first: it does not matter where you have been or what you have done — God wants you to be in a relationship with Him. Even if you believe that you are the worst person who has ever lived and that you have done something unforgivable, God still wants you to be in a relationship with Him. The Bible says that the only thing that God cannot and will not forgive is blasphemy against His Holy Spirit, which I believe is a lifetime spent rejecting God at every turn — unbelief.

Maybe you believe that you have no faults, or that you have never really done anything terribly wrong. No matter what we may choose to believe, the truth is that we have all done wrong. "For all have sinned and fall short of the glory of God" (Romans 3:23). Sins are things we have done wrong. Some people believe they can earn God's love by being good, doing good things, or going to church, but make no mistake — God's love is free; it cannot be earned. That is right: God loves you and wants to be in a relationship with you, but you have to believe. No one can earn heaven. "By grace you have been saved through faith; and that not of yourselves, it is the gift of God; not as a result of works, so that no one may boast" (Ephesians 2:8-9). You cannot work your way into heaven, nor can anyone earn heaven; being with God in heaven can only be obtained through grace by faith. You must believe God and trust in Him! God will not force you to love Him and believe in Him, because then it would not be love. Forced love is not love. God wants to give you an opportunity to learn about Him and then choose for yourself what you will do.

Do you want to begin to live a life filled with purpose and direction? God wants to teach all of us how to live life to the fullest. God wants to fill our lives with good things that will not only bless us but will also bless those around us. Jesus says, "Come to Me, all who are weary and heavy-laden, and I will give you rest. Take My yoke upon you and learn from Me, for I am gentle and humble in heart, and you will find rest for your souls. For My yoke is easy and My burden is light" (Matthew 11:28-30). God is calling each one of us into a relationship with Him. God wants to be a part of your life and to help you find rest and contentment by walking through life with Him.

In saying this, I need to ask for your forgiveness. Yes, that is right — I am asking you, the reader, if you will forgive me and so many others who have come to believe in the one true God. You see, somewhere along the way, we have failed to live the lives that God has called us to. Because of this, we have failed to speak truth into the lives of those around us. In the following pages, I would like to share what we can do to change this sad fact. The mysteries of God have been entrusted to us as believers. These mysteries will set us free — believer and unbeliever alike — and joy, peace, and hope will empower us to love the way God is calling us to love.

If God is love, which the Bible clearly teaches, then His love for us will change and transform us. By learning to love God the way He desires to be loved, we will love others more deeply than we ever could have in our own power. Only a small number of the people of God live the way God has intended, with passion, full of God's power working in and through them. These people have infectious dispositions; and their personalities seem to draw people, because their words are filled with compassion and understanding. They love people and want to share the amazing truth of how God can transform each person's life in a way that not only makes life worth living but makes it exhilarating. The first thing you need to know is this: God loves you.

3

God Loves You!

Remember that God has been right beside you all along. God has been at work in your life, trying to draw you to Himself. The truth is that God loves you more than your finite mind can ever imagine. God loves you more than your mother or father, your children, or anyone else you can think of. This is hard for some to believe; but the way God loves you is stronger than your love for anyone. God loves you more than you love your spouse, your parents, your siblings, or your children. In the book of Jeremiah, God tells Israel, "I have loved you with an everlasting love; therefore I have drawn you with lovingkindness" (Jeremiah 31:3b). He is saying the same thing to you. God loves you with an everlasting love. Since God is love, who better to show us how to love? God loves you so much that He would die in order to prove how great His love is for you. In fact, He did die for you. Jesus willingly laid Himself down on a cross some two thousand years ago, allowed His hands and His feet to be nailed to that cross, and then He suffered and died to prove how great a love He has for you. God died in your place. God, in the person of Jesus Christ, died for all the things that you have ever done wrong. He died for every person that ever lived. He was the ultimate sacrifice for the sins of the world. We serve God the Father, God the Son, and God the Holy Spirit. He is a triune God who is one God. My finite mind cannot totally understand this fact. Without a doubt, I cannot explain God; but we will continue to revisit this as we work through what the Bible teaches us about God.

> God, after He spoke long ago to the fathers in the prophets in many portions and in many ways, in these last days has spoken to us in His Son, whom He appointed heir of all things, through whom also He made the world. And He is the radiance of His glory and the exact representation of His nature, and upholds all things by the word of His power. When He had made purification of sins, He sat down at the right hand of the Majesty on high, having become as much better than the angels, as He has inherited a more excellent name than they (Hebrews 1:1-4).

God Revealed Through Jesus

Jesus, through whom God made the world, left heaven and came to earth to show us who the Father is. And Jesus died on a cross so that our sins could be forgiven and so that we could have fellowship with God through Him. That is the good news — that everything you ever did wrong has been paid for through the death of Jesus Christ on the cross. Not just what you did wrong yesterday and today, but all that you will ever do wrong has been paid for by the death of Jesus. Every sin from the beginning of time until the end of time was nailed to the cross with Jesus. His death paid the price for sin. And the story does not end there, because after Jesus died, God raised Him from the dead; and He is now seated at the right hand of the throne of God with all authority and power given to Him. "In the beginning was the Word, and the Word was with God, and the Word was God. He was in the beginning with God. All things came into being through Him, and apart from Him nothing came into being that has come into being. In Him was life, and the life was the Light of men" (John 1:1-4). Jesus, as God, created everything. It does not matter whether you believe it; it is a fact. Have you ever heard someone say something like this: "God said it and I believe it so that settles it"? In truth, if God said it, then that settles it, whether we believe it or not. God is real whether or not we believe in Him. Just because someone does not believe in God does not negate the fact that He is real.

God is and was and always will be. "'I am the Alpha and the Omega,' says the Lord God, 'who is and who was and who is to come, the Almighty'" (Revelation 1:8). The Almighty God loves you and wants you to love Him. God tells Jeremiah, "Before I formed you in the womb I knew you, and before you were born I consecrated you" (Jeremiah 1:5). This is what God is trying to get us to understand that He knew us even before we were born, and He wants to be our heavenly Father. He wants to consecrate us — to set us apart for His use — and this is possible because of what Jesus has done on the cross. However, it is not possible without faith; we must believe that God is who He says He is and trust Him. God wants to use our lives to demonstrate His love for others. God wants to use us to love people. First, God wants us to love Him, and then He wants us to love those He has put in our lives. God makes us holy and righteous when we choose to believe and trust in Him. Holy means sacred, purified, ready and willing to be used by God. When we choose to love God and believe in Him, God makes us holy and righteous. Righteousness comes through faith, believing and trusting God; and this is how God chooses to see us because of the atoning death of His Son Jesus Christ. And now God wants to fill our lives with joy, peace, and love and to use us to love others with His unconditional love. However, we must first believe. "If you confess with your mouth Jesus as Lord, and believe in your heart that God raised Him from the dead, you will be saved; for with the heart a person believes, resulting in righteousness, and with the mouth he confesses, resulting in salvation" (Romans 10:9-10).

It does not matter what we have or have not done. There is nothing we can do to make God love us more and nothing we can do to make Him love us less. He constantly pursues us to bring us into a right relationship with Him. We are made right by faith, believing that Jesus died for us and confessing that fact. To be "saved" means to be made right with God. God has saved us from eternal separation from Him. God gives us eternal life when we believe in Him. He fills our lives with His Holy Spirit, who brings hope and peace and joy as we begin our lives anew. We can now choose to go through each day filled with His Spirit, cleansed from all sin — everything we have ever done wrong — the sins of our yesterday, our today, and all of our tomorrows have been paid for on the cross. "For the death that He [Jesus] died, He died to sin once for all; but the life He lives, He lives to God. Even so consider yourselves to be dead to sin, but alive to God in Christ Jesus" (Romans 6:10-11).

Christ Jesus died once for all sin. It is because of this fact that we can be set free from the penalty of sin (which is death) and live for God. Living for God is as simple as believing and living a life filled with love for God and for people. Choose to love. How does it make you feel, being called to live a life filled with love? In truth, it is what we all desire. We want to be loved just as we are, with all our faults and failures. This is how God loves us — with His unconditional love. It does not matter how many times we have failed Him or how much we have done wrong. God loves us! Does knowing this make you want to learn to love people the way you want to be loved?

The Power Within

What would the world be like if we decided to live in a way that helped people everywhere succeed? What if we were more concerned that those around us had everything they needed to live life? Can you imagine what the world would be like if people everywhere were working together to make this world a better place? I think it would be called heaven. Jesus has made heaven possible just by believing in Him and in God the Father, trusting in Him, and receiving all that He wants to give us. "For this is the will of My Father, that everyone who beholds the Son and believes in Him will have eternal life, and I Myself will raise him up on the last day" (John 6:40). The Bible teaches us that Jesus died so that we can live. Jesus died in order to bring us into a right relationship with the triune God. Jesus died so that we could be filled with His Spirit, who will empower us to love. Jesus tells us,

> I will ask the Father, and He will give you another Helper, that He may be with you forever; that is the Spirit of truth, whom the world cannot receive, because it does not see Him or know Him, but you know Him because He abides with you and will be in you. I will not leave you as orphans; I will come to you. After a little while the world will no longer see Me, but you will see Me; because I live, you will live also. In that day you will know that I am in My

Father, and you in Me, and I in you. He who has My commandments and keeps them is the one who loves Me; and he who loves Me will be loved by My Father, and I will love him and will disclose Myself to him (John 14:16-21).

Once we choose to believe and place our faith in God because of the finished work of Jesus Christ on the cross, the Holy Spirit of the triune God dwells in us. This is how we know that we have made the right choice, because the Holy Spirit dwells in us and reveals to us that we belong to God. The same Spirit that raised Jesus Christ from the dead comes to dwell in us and teach us to love God and to love others. When we choose to believe that God loves us, then we need to get to know Him; and reading the Bible gives us great insight into the heart of the living God. We can get to know Him on a deep and personal level by reading His Word; and now that we believe, God's Holy Spirit will reveal deep and secret things to us through the Word of God.

4

How Do We Know The Bible Is True?

The Bible, God's Word, is His love letter to us, and it has some stories that will speak love directly into your heart. The sad thing is that few people have ever read the Bible from cover to cover. If you have not read the Bible and studied the pages of this holy book, then you have no right to say things you have heard, like "the Bible has been changed over and over again." "The Bible is not really relevant for us today." "How can we trust what the Bible teaches?" The most important fact to remember is that God says His Word will stand forever; and since God said this, that settles it. For those who are still skeptical and need proof, keep reading. These are questions we can answer by looking at what God says in His Word and historical facts.

Let us first look to the Scriptures; if we believe in God, then it would follow that we believe in the Bible, which is God's Holy Word. Peter tells us, "But know this first of all, that no prophecy of Scripture is a matter of one's own interpretation, for no prophecy was ever made by an act of human will, but men moved by the Holy Spirit spoke from God" (2 Peter 1:20-21). What this tells us is that even though the Bible was written through the hands of men, God's Holy Spirit was telling them what to write. We hear Jesus telling us this long before Peter's letter. In the Gospel of John, Jesus says, "But when He, the Spirit of truth, comes, He will guide you into all truth; for He will not speak on His own initiative, but whatever He hears, He will speak; and He will disclose to you what is to come" (John 16:13). The Holy Spirit of God continues to do this even today. God speaks to us through His Word in the power of His Holy Spirit. Once you become a believer (a follower of Christ), God will begin to speak to you through His Word every time you open the Bible wanting to learn more about Him. Even reading the Bible as an unbeliever, God can still speak to you; but we need to be reminded that unbelief is the greatest sin, since unbelief says there is no God. The Bible tells us that the Scriptures are foolishness to those who do not believe because the Scriptures are spiritually discerned. Without the Holy Spirit, the Bible is not comprehensible. When we have chosen to believe in and trust Him, God's Holy Spirit comes into our lives to teach us and give us understanding of the deep and secret mysteries of God. Even now, after reading and studying the Bible for over twenty years, there are still parts I do not understand. The apostle Peter said that Paul wrote things that are hard to understand, so I just continue to read, study, and pray asking for understanding.

> What we have received is not the spirit of the world, but the Spirit who is from God, so that we may understand what God has freely given us. This is what we speak, not in words taught us by human wisdom but in words taught by the Spirit, explaining spiritual realities with Spirit-taught words. The person without

> the Spirit does not accept the things that come from
> the Spirit of God but considers them foolishness, and
> cannot understand them because they are discerned
> only through the Spirit. (1 Corinthians 2:12-14 NIV).

If we believe in God, His Spirit not only dwells in us but also guides us, teaches us, comforts us, convicts us of things done wrong and things done right. God wants to be a part of every facet of our lives, helping us as we walk through each day, giving us direction and insight. God uses His Word to point the way. Paul tells us, "All Scripture is inspired by God and profitable for teaching, for reproof, for correction, for training in righteousness; so that the man of God may be adequate, equipped for every good work" (2 Timothy 3:16-17). I love the way the Living Bible translates these verses:

> The whole Bible was given to us by inspiration from
> God and is useful to teach us what is true and to make
> us realize what is wrong in our lives; it straightens
> us out and helps us do what is right. It is God's way
> of making us well prepared at every point, fully
> equipped to do good to everyone.

Historical Fact

In 1964 a great discovery was made in the Qumran caves on the northwest shore of the Dead Sea — a group of ancient documents known as the Dead Sea Scrolls. The scrolls are copies of several books of the Bible. They are dated from around 150 BC to 70 AD; and when they are compared to modern day translations, they are the same. One of the scrolls they were able to preserve is the complete book of Isaiah, which is the largest book in the Bible which is sixty six chapters. The complete book of Isaiah, written more than 2000 years ago — and when put alongside our modern translations it is the same, word for word. I hope the verses that have been shared from God's Word and the finding of scrolls hidden away in obscure caves will help you believe.

God is waiting for you to make a commitment of faith, to receive the Spirit of God, who is waiting to show you great and mighty things you have never known and never will know without Him dwelling in you. "The grass withers, the flower fades, but the word of our God stands forever" (Isaiah 40:8). The Word of God will endure, will stand, will be around, and will be relevant forever! The Bible is God's way of speaking to us and teaching us more about Him. I know without a doubt that the God I serve is able to write a book through the hands of sinful men and not only make it relevant for every generation but to keep it just the way He wrote it from the time the first author penned the first word until today and even until forever.

If you really want to know God and you really want to have great wisdom, then read your Bible and pray. As you read God's Word, ask Him to open your eyes to see Him — He will reveal Himself to you through the Scriptures. Ask God to open your ears to hear Him — He will speak to you through the Scriptures. Ask God to open your mind to be changed about Him — He will reveal His truth to you. Ask God to open your heart so you can receive and believe the truths He has shared with you, and your life will be changed forever. This is what is called fellowship with God. When we pray, we are sharing our hearts with God; when we read the Bible, God is sharing His heart with us. This is a two-sided conversation. If you are not studying the Scriptures daily, then your wisdom is from the world and skewed by the world. If you trust in worldly wisdom that is not from God, it will leave you empty, confused, and depressed. "The wisdom of this world is foolishness before God" (1 Corinthians 3:19a). "Since in the wisdom of God the world through its wisdom did not come to know God, God was well pleased through the foolishness of the message preached to save those who believe" (1 Corinthians 1:21). Worldly wisdom says there is no God, and just look at the mess our world is in.

Relevant

The world says the Bible is old and not relevant for today. As for relevance, you tell me. Is "do not kill" still relevant today? Or "Do not steal," or "Do not lie," or "Do not bear false witness," or "Honor your mother and father"? What about God's command to love — is that still relevant today? I believe everyone wants and deserves to be loved. The Bible can teach us timeless truths that fill our hearts with joy and peace. God uses the Bible to teach us how to live life to the fullest. God's Word was written by the hand of God for us. How can it not be relevant for every generation? There are many truths found in the pages of Scripture that need to be incorporated into our daily lives — truths which, when put in practice, will set you free. Jesus says, "If you continue in My word, then you are truly disciples of Mine; and you will know the truth, and the truth will make you free" (John 8:31b-32). Something we do not realize is that when we are living against the rules of God, we are not only hurting ourselves but those around us as well. But when we live our lives according to the rules that God has given rules that protect us and others, life can be wonderful. Living life filled with love can be exciting.

Think about it: good friends are hard to come by; and when we find good friends, we want to be around them, go places with them, and do things with them so we can spend time together. One sure way of finding good friends is by being a good friend. Loving God and loving people equals loving life. Does just knowing that God's love for you is unconditional make your heart sing? This truth is worth sharing again. There is nothing that you can do to make God love you more and nothing you can do to make God love you less. God loves you; and if you were the only person of His creation, God would still give His life for you. God loves you and wants you to get to know Him. It is in His Word that we read the following verse:

> 'For I know the plans that I have for you,' declares the Lord, 'plans for welfare and not for calamity to give you a future and a hope. Then you will call upon Me and come and pray to Me, and I will listen to you. You will seek Me and find Me when you search for Me with all your heart' (Jeremiah 29:11-13).

Does this sound relevant to you? Does it move you to action? Do you want to know and understand the God of the universe? God already knows you, because He created you. God knows you more intimately than you know yourself. Now God wants you to know Him, to seek Him and understand Him. What is the one thing that we need more than any other thing in life? Love! We want to be loved; well, so does God. God wants to be loved by His creation. God wants us to love Him and be in a relationship with Him, so He gives us unconditional love to teach us how to love Him and others. God wants us to choose love, to love because we choose it, not because we have to.

The Mysteries of God

God has given us great and wonderful promises that can make life more fulfilling, even exciting, when we choose to live by the law of love. When we choose love as our guiding light, the God of love entrusts us with the mysteries of God. "Let a man regard us in this manner, as servants of Christ and stewards of the mysteries" (1 Corinthians 4:1). These mysteries are hidden truths found in the promises of God. When we choose to live life with the high calling of God on our lives, these truths will become evident to us and will help us in our walk with God. Walking with God is simply trusting Him to be our helper as we go through each day. He will direct us, teach us, and give us wisdom if we will allow Him. God will also help us as we minister to people, lost and saved alike. These mysteries are hard to explain but it is what God does when we choose to obey. Once we choose obedience, something miraculous happens that can only be attributed to God and His mighty power working in and through us. I will try to explain in the following chapters.

5

Spending Time Alone with God

The most important thing we can do to get to know God is to read the Bible. The Bible is the primary way God speaks to us. He can also speak to us through our circumstances, through nature, through other people, and in other ways. However, God will speak to us each and every day through His Word if we will let Him. God even teaches us how important His Word is for daily living.

> My child, if you will receive my words and treasure my commandments within you, make your ear attentive to wisdom, incline your heart to understanding; for if you cry for discernment, lift your voice for understanding; if you seek her as silver and search for her as for hidden treasures; then you will discern the fear of the Lord and discover the knowledge of God. For the Lord gives wisdom; from His mouth come knowledge and understanding. He stores up sound wisdom for the upright; He is a shield to those who walk in integrity, guarding the paths of justice, and He preserves the way of His godly ones. Then

you will discern righteousness and justice and equity and every good course. For wisdom will enter your heart and knowledge will be pleasant to your soul; discretion will guard you, understanding will watch over you, to deliver you from the way of evil, from the man who speaks perverse things; from those who leave the paths of uprightness to walk in the ways of darkness (Proverbs 2:1-13).

This is God's goal for our lives. When we spend time reading and studying it, the Word of God will teach us how we are supposed to live. It will empower us to change, it will convict us of things we have done wrong and also of things we have done right. God's Word will correct us by showing us God's way and will equip us with the tools we need to succeed in life according to God's principles. Most of all, as we study God's Word, we will learn more about who God is.

God's way of correcting us is not by shaking His finger in our faces or slapping us around whenever we fail. If this is your picture of God, you need a new picture. A former pastor of mine says that God pulls us close and deals with us in His hug. God will work with us in a loving way. Try that the next time you have to discipline your child. Pull them in and hug them, then tell them what you believe they did wrong and lovingly work through the problem. You will not believe the response you will get. As earthly mothers and fathers, sometimes our discipline is too harsh, sometimes not harsh enough, and at other times nonexistent — all of which do harm. Many of us can think of times when the discipline we received bordered on abuse. God is just not that way. God's discipline is not harsh. Our circumstances may be harsh or the situation out of our control, but make no mistake — God patiently waits for us to turn to Him and respond to Him in love. Remember, if we never accept God's free gift of love and never turn to Him through repentance or ask Him to guide us through life, the consequences will be very harsh. Repentance means to change directions, like an about-face. It means if you do not believe in God, then change directions and choose to believe. It can also mean if you are doing something that you know is wrong, then stop, and start doing what you know is right. If you do not believe in God and are teaching others to do the same, then you need to change what you believe. Rejecting God for all of life is saying to God, "I do not need you now, and I will never need You." God will honor that request and allow you to spend eternity without Him in a spiritual prison called hell. It is hell because God's presence is not there. God does not send people to hell; but if we choose to live without Him, God will honor our choice.

God Blesses Obedience

I have chosen to believe in God now, and I am learning about how great a love He has for me. I experience His presence and power in my daily life. Walking through life believing that I am some rough, tough, self-made man who can get through this life on my own is quite arrogant. I have already lived like that long enough; and God knows the years of hurt and pain and devastation I have left behind due to living life under my own power, by my own system of beliefs. However, that was then, and this is now. I have read the Bible numerous times, and each time I learn more about God. Each time I am drawn closer to Him. I love His Word, and I know it is because of my obedience to read and study that God has increased my love for Him and for others. David says, in Psalm 119:11, "Your word I have treasured in my heart that I may not sin against You."

David knew that by having God's Word hidden in his heart (memorized) would help him to avoid doing things wrong. God tells Joshua, "This book of the law shall not depart from your mouth, but you shall meditate on it day and night, so that you may be careful to do according to all that is written in it; for then you will make your way prosperous, and then you will have success" (Joshua 1:8). Notice the promises at the end of this verse. God is telling us to obey and be blessed. The miraculous thing is that God's Word increases our faith and helps us have godly desires. When we spend time with God in His Word, we find our faith being increased; we begin to fall more in love with God, and we find our desires beginning to change. "For it is God who is at work in you, both to will and to work for His good pleasure" (Philippians 2:13).

Obedience and worship will become our desire. We will want to please God. Then God will continue to encourage us, convict us, teach us, and change us through His Word. "For the Word of God is alive and active. Sharper than any double-edged sword, it penetrates even to dividing soul and spirit, joints and marrow; it judges the thoughts and attitudes of the heart" (Hebrews 4:12 NIV). The Word of God is able to pierce our hearts and penetrate our deepest thoughts and desires. God's Word can help us change some of the vilest practices and remove the most hateful thoughts, filling our hearts with joy and our minds with peace. God's Word will help us to focus on the promises of God, promises that tell us that God is able to deliver us from anything, no matter the situation or the circumstances. There is nothing that God cannot do to deliver us from the problems we are facing, the sin we have fallen into, or the sickness that has overwhelmed us. "Trust in the Lord with all your heart and do not lean on your own understanding. In all your ways acknowledge Him, and He will make your paths straight" (Proverbs 3:5-6). "Do not fear, for I am with you; do not anxiously look about you, for I am your God. I will strengthen you, surely I will help you, surely I will uphold you with My righteous right hand" (Isaiah 41:10). Do these verses give you hope? Throughout the Bible God is telling us that He wants to be involved in every area of our lives. God wants to walk with us, talk with us and pour His love out on us. Are you willing to let God do this? It takes commitment, dedication, and perseverance; but God will give us what it takes if we are willing to seek Him diligently. You can find God revealing Himself to you throughout the Scriptures if you are willing to commit to a daily time alone with God by praying and reading His Word. It is a time that you will have to guard and protect; because once you start, the devil will entice you with many things to make you stop this most holy time of Biblical study. Without a doubt, this time alone with God will prepare you for whatever may come.

> My child, if you will receive my words and treasure my commandments within you, make your ear attentive to wisdom, incline your heart to understanding; for if you cry for discernment, lift your voice for understanding; if you seek her as silver and search for her as for hidden treasures; then you will discern the fear of the Lord and discover the knowledge of God (Proverbs 2:1-7).

Wow! What a promise! You will discover the knowledge of God.

Have You Been Forgotten?

In the book of Jeremiah God tells the prophet, "My people have forgotten Me days without number" (Jeremiah 2:32b).

How sad is that? God's own creation has forgotten its creator. How would you feel if those you love the most forgot you? How would you feel if those you loved did not want anything to do with you? It makes me sad just to think about it. But God also tells us in this same book to "Call to Me and I will answer you, and I will tell you great and mighty things, which you do not know" (Jeremiah 33:3). God wants us to be in fellowship with Him. This means that we tell God our hearts' desires, even though He already knows; and God tells us His heart's desires as we spend time in His Holy Word. This type of fellowship puts us into conversation with God.

God goes on to say, "'Let him who boasts boast of this, that he understands and knows Me, that I am the Lord who exercises lovingkindness, justice and righteousness on earth; for I delight in these things,' declares the Lord" (Jeremiah 9:24). God is telling us here that we can know and understand Him. I know our understanding of God is limited, but wow! Just knowing that God wants us to understand Him should drive us to seek Him in the way He desires to be sought. We can understand and know God more by reading the Bible. The Bible is God's love letter, written to mankind for the purpose of knowing and understanding God's heart. We begin walking with God by doing two things. The first is reading His words to us in the Bible, and the second is talking with God. When our thoughts purposefully return to God throughout each day, we are walking in fellowship with Him. Thinking about God, believing in God, praising God, and talking to God (prayer) are known as fellowship. This is how we have a personal, intimate relationship with the Creator of the universe. When we spend time in God's Word each day, we are saying, "I love you, God, and I want to know you more." God will speak to us through His Word.

I believe that the polls saying 85% of Americans are Christians are wrong. Maybe somewhere between 12% and 15% of Americans are truly Bible-believing, born again, Spirit-filled believers in Jesus Christ. Of that percentage, I wonder how many have developed a time alone with God? I know the percentage of that poll would break my heart, and it does break God's heart each and every day. God longs to be part of our lives, and there is an innate desire within each of us to be known by Him. We can find all kinds of things to take up our time; but it all leaves us empty, dissatisfied, and wanting more. That is because only God can make us complete and fulfill our hearts' desires. What we do not realize is that our souls cry out for God, but we fill our lives with so many things that God's still, small voice is drowned out. Jeremiah, the weeping prophet, was told by God not to pray any longer for His people, because they had turned their backs on God in order to serve gods made of wood and covered with silver and gold. They were serving idols that could not hear, that could not speak, and that could not satisfy. How many things are we giving our time to that cannot hear, cannot speak, or cannot satisfy? Pick up your Bible, spend some time alone with the Creator of the universe, and see if your life is not changed by Him.

Great and Magnificent Promises

How amazing is it that God used around forty authors to write the Bible and they all are teaching us about God, His greatness, His power, and His desire for us. The following verses teach us about God and His desire for us.

> Simon Peter, a bond-servant and apostle of Jesus Christ, to those who have received a faith of the same kind as ours, by the righteousness of our God and

Savior, Jesus Christ: Grace and peace be multiplied to you in the knowledge of God and of Jesus our Lord; seeing that His divine power has granted to us everything pertaining to life and godliness, through the true knowledge of Him who called us by His own glory and excellence. For by these He has granted to us His precious and magnificent promises, so that by them you may become partakers of the divine nature, having escaped the corruption that is in the world by lust (2 Peter 1:1-4).

What great and magnificent promises — eternal life, heaven, partaking of the divine nature, knowledge of God, and, best of all, His presence. God has chosen us and is calling us to Himself. He wants to reveal more of Himself to us through His Word, if we will just spend time alone with Him each day.

For you have been born again not of seed which is perishable but imperishable, that is, through the living and enduring word of God (1 Peter 1:23).

For this reason we also constantly thank God that when you received the word of God which you heard from us, you accepted it not as the word of men, but for what it really is, the word of God, which also performs its work in you who believe (1 Thessalonians 2:13).

For whatever was written in earlier times was written for our instruction, so that through perseverance and the encouragement of the Scriptures we might have hope. Now may the God who gives perseverance and encouragement grant you to be of the same mind with one another according to Christ Jesus, so that with one accord you may with one voice glorify the God and Father of our Lord Jesus Christ (Romans 15:4-6).

These have been written so that you may believe that Jesus is the Christ, the Son of God; and that believing you may have life in His name (John 20:31).

God wants to do a work in our hearts and make us more like Him. If you really want to live life to the fullest, if you really want to make the most of your life, give your life to God. Live your life for Him. If you already are a believer, then spend time alone with God each day reading His Word. Every time you open your Bible, you are saying, "God, I love you and I want to know you more." Each time you open your Bible, bow your head to read, and receive what God has for you, that is worship.

6

Prayer

Praying is another way to say, "God, I believe in you and I trust you." God wants us to pray because many times He will show us what we really need as we spend time sharing our needs with Him. Prayer is intended to grow our faith, as we see God answering our prayers and encouraging us during times of prayer. Many times when we pray, God will bring a verse or a portion of Scripture to mind, and that is the most direct way we can hear God's voice. When I am asking God for a specific need or help in a situation or circumstance and He brings a verse to my mind, it is the answer I need to hear. It could be a word of encouragement or hope, guidance, direction, teaching, or conviction. God will convict us of things we have done wrong and of things we have done right. Prayer is how we talk with God, and God uses His Word to talk with us. We can also remind God of His promises when we pray; but if we are not students of His Word, how will we know His promises? How will we know God? It is impossible to get to know someone without spending time with them.

Our strongest human relationships are made strong by time spent with each other. It is the same with God; the only difference is that we are bowing before the Most High God. This is the most important relationship in our lives, because God is love. When I grow in my love for God, my love for others grows as well. Then, our prayers even begin to change as our focus shifts from praying for self to praying for others. We need to pray for ourselves, but we also need to pray for others. Is it possible that we could be the only ones praying for our loved ones? I have often wondered who was praying for me during the hardest times in my life. Or who was praying for me when I chose not to believe in God? I know without a doubt that God had me on the mind of believers praying for me. Even though I was choosing to live a life of unbelief, God never gave up on me. God chose to believe in me. He is my creator. Wow — what a revelation! God is your creator, too, whether you believe it or not.

For this reason alone, our attitude in prayer needs to be one of thankfulness. "Devote yourselves to prayer, keeping alert in it with an attitude of thanksgiving" (Colossians 4:2). If God has not answered my prayer in the way I think He should, I need to be ready to accept "no" or "wait" as an answer. When I follow God's direction, there is no place for worry or anxiety to creep in; and when it tries, I can meditate on God's promises. I sing songs of praise that remind me of who God is, His greatness, what He has done in my life, what He is doing, and what He will continue to do. When I place my faith in God and trust Him, I know He is doing His perfect work in my life and in the lives of those for whom He has me praying. "The end of all things is near; therefore, be of sound judgment and sober spirit for the purpose of prayer. Above all, keep fervent in your love for one another, because love covers a multitude of sins" (1 Peter 4:7-8). I have to choose to believe His Word and not what I see. Just because it does not seem like God is getting through to those

I am praying for does not mean that He is not at work in their lives. It means I have to trust Him and remember what He has promised all of us who stand on His promises. "This is the confidence which we have before Him, that, if we ask anything according to His will, He hears us. And if we know that He hears us in whatever we ask, we know that we have the requests which we have asked from Him" (1 John 5:14-15). This is just one of the many great promises of God found in the Bible. This verse encourages me and moves me to action, especially when it seems like everything and everyone are against me. When my world is falling apart and those that I love are not living life the way they should, I know that God is at work in their lives and mine because of His promises to me. So I choose to trust Him; even though I cannot see His hand moving, I can trust that He is. We also need to realize that God is praying for us.

> In the same way the Spirit also helps our weakness; for we do not know how to pray as we should, but the Spirit Himself intercedes for us with groanings too deep for words; and He who searches the hearts knows what the mind of the Spirit is, because He intercedes for the saints according to the will of God (Romans 8:26-27).

> Who is the one who condemns? Christ Jesus is He who died, yes, rather who was raised, who is at the right hand of God, who also intercedes for us (Romans 8:34).

> Jesus, on the other hand, because He continues forever, holds His priesthood permanently. Therefore He is able also to save forever those who draw near to God through Him, since He always lives to make intercession for them (Hebrews 7:24-25).

These verses fill my heart with such joy that I cannot even contain myself. The knowledge gained here is so wonderful and more awesome than we can ever realize. Just think about what these verses are saying. They are teaching us that the Lord of lords and the King of kings, who is seated at the right hand of the throne of God, will never cease making intercession (prayer) for us. Jesus never ceases to make intercession for us. Wow! Then add to this magnificent and precious promise the knowledge that the Holy Spirit of the Living God prays for us (the saints) according to the will of God. As the psalmist would say, "Such knowledge is too wonderful for me; it is too high, I cannot attain to it" (Psalm 139:6).

> "Be anxious for nothing, but in everything by prayer and supplication with thanksgiving let your requests be made known to God. And the peace of God, which surpasses all comprehension, will guard your hearts and your minds in Christ Jesus" (Philippians 4:6-7).

This is another great and magnificent promise — that "the peace of God which surpasses all comprehension will guard our hearts and minds in Christ Jesus" (Philippians 4:7). If we have an attitude of thanksgiving, we are telling God that we trust Him, since we know by faith God has our best interest at heart. God knows what we need before we ask Him, but He wants us to realize what our needs truly are. Many times we ask God for things we want but don't necessarily need. Some of the things we are asking God for could hurt us in the long run, and so God answers that prayer in a way that will move us to a place of growth if we trust Him. "Rejoice always; pray without ceasing; in everything give thanks; for this is God's will for you in Christ Jesus" (1 Thessalonians 5:16-18).

In Everything Give Thanks

There are some things in my life that are really hard to be thankful for — but God tells me to be thankful. Some things in life are truly difficult to endure — but there is always one sure thing that we can be thankful for: God's presence. God was there with us and is still with us. He has the power to help us to overcome anything, if we will only choose to let go and let Him heal us. Being unthankful is being unholy. Living life without thankfulness will lead us to a deep place of darkness. We begin to concentrate on all that is negative, harmful and depressing. Our focus changes from being centered on God and all that is good to being distracted by dire circumstances. We get to choose to fix our attention on God or on our situation. We can meditate on all that is detrimental or on the God who is in control of our situation and circumstances. "And we know that God causes all things to work together for good to those who love God, to those who are called according to His purpose" (Romans 8:28). God causes all things to work together for good — that means the good, the bad, and the ugly. Therein lies a mystery: God can use all our faults, our failures, and even those ugly things that have been done against us for our good if we will trust Him. Our faith must be in the One True God working in our lives, helping us overcome our faults and failures, helping us to forgive others, and helping us to choose love even when someone is unlovable.

> If you love those who love you, what credit is that to you? For even sinners love those who love them. If you do good to those who do good to you, what credit is that to you? For even sinners do the same. If you lend to those from whom you expect to receive, what credit is that to you? Even sinners lend to sinners in

order to receive back the same amount. But love your enemies, and do good, and lend, expecting nothing in return; and your reward will be great, and you will be sons of the Most High; for He Himself is kind to ungrateful and evil men. Be merciful, just as your Father is merciful (Luke 6:32-36).

Here is another mystery. God tells us to love the unlovable — even those who have used us, persecuted us, abused us. It is impossible for us to do this without God's power. "Now to Him who is able to do far more abundantly beyond all that we ask or think, according to the power that works within us, to Him be the glory in the church and in Christ Jesus to all generations forever and ever. Amen" (Ephesians 3:20-21). God wants to help us to be more than conquerors by His power working in and through us, but we have to ask for His power and be willing to obey by forgiving and choosing to love. An unforgiving spirit will hinder our prayers. Sin will hinder our prayers. But God is faithful, even when we are not. "For the eyes of the Lord are toward the righteous, and His ears attend to their prayer, but the face of the Lord is against those who do evil" (1 Peter 3:12). Evil usually involves hurting others. Our sin hurts others, not just ourselves. Refusal to forgive hurts; hate hurts; being condescending to others hurts; pride hurts. No matter how minor it may seem, usually what we do wrong will have a negative effect on those we are supposed to love. God tells men that when we do not honor our wives, our prayers are hindered. "You husbands in the same way, live with your wives in an understanding way, as with someone weaker, since she is a woman; and show her honor as a fellow heir of the grace of life, so that your prayers will not be hindered" (1 Peter 3:7).

Life is hard enough and there are enough people out there against us. The last person I want working against me is God. I want God to hear my prayers, answer my prayers, and bless my life. So I pray. I pray when I am in the shower. I pray when I am walking my dog. I pray when I am driving, when I am in line at the grocery or at the bank, or wherever I may be found idly standing by. I also look for a quiet place to pray and be alone with God so I can focus. When God brings a person to mind, I know He is leading me to pray for that person. I am not supposed to wonder how they are doing when they come to mind, God is leading me to pray for them. So I pray. Whenever I choose to live in obedience to God, His power to complete the task His power is released into my life. "For I am confident of this very thing, that He who began a good work in you will perfect it until the day of Christ Jesus" (Philippians 1:6). God will continue to work in us and through us if we will allow Him.

7

Higher Calling

All of the things we have been talking about come from a desire to please God. We can please God by choosing to believe in Him. We can please God by obeying His commandments, even though we will fail daily. We can please God by choosing to love Him and love others. Choosing to love is obeying God, who has called us to be obedient and wants to empower us to live a life of obedience to Him. This means choosing the right way all the time, no matter how difficult. In fact, the more difficult life may become, the greater our need to ask God for His power. There are times in our lives when we need the supernatural power of God to keep us from sin.

I need to confess right here and now that I have broken all of God's commandments at one time or another, and most of them many times over. I have committed adultery in my heart countless times. I have murdered by hate (not the physical act) often. I grew up being a habitual liar with a mischievous heart. I walked against God until I was 31, and even after becoming a Christian I have fallen into the trap of sin more times than I can count. I feel like one of the greatest failures and the worst sinner of all time. I know firsthand how terrible life can be when I let sin rule instead of learning to be filled with the Holy Spirit of God. I have come a long way in my more than twenty years of being a Christian, but I still struggle with being obedient. I also know it is the same with all of us: we will fall and we will fail, but as we continue to look to Jesus and rely on the power that raised Him from the dead instead of on our own strength, we will become more than conquerors. "The steps of a man are established by the Lord, and He delights in his way. When he falls, he will not be hurled headlong, because the Lord is the One who holds his hand" (Psalm 37:23-24). God is a merciful God who loves us and chooses to be our help if we will but let Him.

> The Lord is compassionate and gracious, slow to anger and abounding in lovingkindness. He will not always strive with us, nor will He keep His anger forever. He has not dealt with us according to our sins, nor rewarded us according to our iniquities. For as high as the heavens are above the earth, so great is His lovingkindness toward those who fear Him. As far as the east is from the west, so far has He removed our transgressions from us. Just as a father has compassion on his children, so the Lord has compassion on those who fear him. For He Himself knows our frame; He is mindful that we are but dust (Psalm 103:8-14).

God is such an awesome God that He chooses to do whatever it takes to bring us near to Him. God even wants to help us with our past, which will fall by the wayside if we will allow it, and fill our hearts and lives with joy. Peace will rule our lives. Hope will shine in and through us. People will be drawn to us, and we will bring glory to God as we minister to those who are hurting and begin to disciple them to be followers of Christ.

We lay down the hurt, pain, and sorrow, pick up our crosses, and look to Jesus to show us the way. We can choose to be filled with peace instead of anger or anxiety. We can choose to love instead of hate. "Everyone who hates his brother is a murderer; and you know that no murderer has eternal life abiding in him" (1 John 3:15). Hate is a learned behavior and is murder according to God's higher calling — but love overcomes hate. Read 1 John — it is a small book devoted to teaching us how to love. The Bible says that "love covers a multitude of sins" (1st Peter 4:8b). When we choose to forgive and to love, a multitude of sins are being covered. Choosing to love honors God and it is worship. It is not natural to love the way God wants us to love. It is something supernatural, and without the presence and power of God in our lives, it is simply not possible. It is not possible to live our lives according to the higher calling God has on our lives without total dependence on Him.

Love Allows Pain to Exist

There are times our lives are filled with suffering. It could be from the loss of a loved one, from bad choices we or those we love have made, from any number of things. The point I want to make is that sometimes love allows pain to exist. Christ on the cross is one example of this. Tough love is another; discipline is love allowing pain to exist. Allowing your children to fail is a choice made through love. Choosing to love someone who has hurt you is painful, but necessary in order to demonstrate the unconditional love of God. Choosing to forgive is painful. You may get tired of hearing that, but I want to continue to drive this point home. If I choose to love and spend time with someone, learn to listen to them, and ask God to help me to love them the way they need to be loved, then I am living in obedience to God's command. This demonstrates my desire to live according to the high calling of God on my life. Worship! I am sacrificing what I want in order to meet the need of my mate, my child, my sibling, or even my enemy. Are you choosing to love your enemies, or are you talking badly about them, running them down, and using them as an excuse for gossip? Do we constantly run down those who have caused us pain? Or do we relive our abuses or the abuse we endured? This is not what God wants for us.

Just how deep is your love? Are you trying to love in your own power or are you calling on God, asking Him to fill you with the power of His Holy Spirit? "But if the Spirit of Him who raised Jesus from the dead dwells in you, He who raised Christ Jesus from the dead will also give life to your mortal bodies through His Spirit who dwells in you" (Romans 8:11). Wow — the power of God in us! Calling on the power of God is asking for a supernatural love to be demonstrated in and through us. It takes a lot more strength and character to choose love than to choose hate. Hate is easy, natural, a tool of the enemy; God is love. You choose. Either way, we will suffer: either as hate destroys us or as God empowers us to choose love, forgiveness, and reconciliation. Suffering through hate destroys us; suffering by choosing God's way brings life, love, and the power of an Almighty God. Without the power of God's Holy Spirit, living God's way is impossible. God wants to be included in every area of our lives — we are that important to Him.

Christianity is Not For the Faint of Heart

God is calling people to be a part of His church who will inspire others by their desire to worship Him in spirit and truth. In most churches, you will find only a few people who are faithful not because they feel obligated, not because someone is making them go, or because they are trying to do the right thing, but because they want to be found in God's house worshipping Him. These people want to be among other believers who encourage and even inspire others. Corporate worship does just that: it inspires, encourages, and even refreshes believers. This is the way God wants to be worshipped. This is what He tells us: "An hour is coming, and now is, when the true worshipers will worship the Father in spirit and truth; for such people the Father seeks to be His worshipers. God is spirit, and those who worship Him must worship in spirit and truth" (John 4:23-24). If this is what God desires of us, then it is something we need to learn to do, asking God to help us in this great endeavor.

Does it excite you to know that God is specific in how we should worship Him? Does it move you to action? Is it your desire to be pleasing to God, to give God what He wants? This is exactly the type of person God is drawing to Himself: one with a thankful heart, a mind made up to be pleasing in His sight, and a spirit that knows fellowship with God is the only way to have a life of fulfillment and purpose. True worship is intoxicating. Remember, we will fail and we will fall; but God wants us to worship Him in spite of our weaknesses, faults, and shortcomings.

God is looking for people who are excited because they *get* to go to church — not that they *have* to go, but that they *get* to go. They already have hearts filled with worship and have spent time alone each day with God the Father, walking in fellowship with Him. These people are serious about their faith, know the spiritual gifts God has entrusted to them, and are working to edify the church through these gifts. They are already serious students of the Word of God, studying, memorizing, and meditating on the Scriptures. They have developed a love for God and for His Word. You will not find them going days without spending time alone with God in His Word and in prayer. These people have thankful hearts filled with love for their Creator and are intentional about their relationship with Him. They guard the time they spend alone with God each day — nothing and no one can tear them away from meeting with Almighty God, the Creator of the universe. They know all of this is necessary for their spiritual lives, understanding that it is God's will for them to fellowship with Him throughout each day. They choose to be alone with God — a time of being on holy ground, of meeting with a holy God, of refreshing; a time for God to fill them up again with His Holy Spirit. "You will make known to me the path of life; in Your presence is fullness of joy; in Your right hand there are pleasures forever" (Psalm 16:11). They understand that it is not possible to grow spiritually without a daily time alone with God. These people recognize that God loves them and has called them to Himself.

When we finally understand that God first loved us and respond to Him, then we will began to understand the true meaning of unconditional love. We can work toward experiencing and demonstrating that true love. God's love for us compels us to love Him, but not until we begin to walk with God each day does His love begin to change us. It is God's love that makes us better parents, siblings, children, friends. Because God is love and teaches us how to love, we become better people. We lose all bitterness, hate, resentment, jealousy, and a host of other infectious ailments that have marred our lives. We give up being critical, judgmental, overbearing, and demanding. The fruit of the Spirit begins to be seen in our lives: ". . . love, joy, peace, patience, kindness, goodness, faithfulness, gentleness, self-control; against such things there is no law"

(Galatians 5:22-23). Notice how the fruit of the Spirit seem to follow a certain progression. Love of God produces joy, which is followed by His peace. Do you have a heart filled with love? If you do, then you should also have a heart filled with joy and peace.

Patience follows love, joy, and peace — knowing just how patient God has been with me compels me to be patient with others. When my heart is filled with love, joy, and peace, I cannot help but be patient. Patience is not something we should need to pray for, since it is the fruit of the Spirit. If we are walking filled with the Spirit of God, then patience naturally flows from our hearts. We choose to be patient. "But I say, walk by the Spirit, and you will not carry out the desire of the flesh" (Galatians 5:16). It is a check in our spirits that says "Stop" — be patient, or lose your joy and peace and become anxious and filled with anger. Remember that the next time you get cut off in traffic or the next time someone says something really demeaning about you. Remember that when your child is out of control or another loved one is not being very loving. Remember that when you choose to focus on your past instead of on God, things eternal, or things of beauty. Can love win out, or will impatience or self-pity? Does it matter what others think of you, or do you believe what God says about you? God says that because of what Jesus did on the cross, we are now saints and priests, ministers of reconciliation. God says that we are children of the King. We are royalty.

When we choose to be patient and wait, all anxiety will fall away; because we are saying, "I do not know why this is happening, but I trust you, Lord." When we choose to be patient with others, we have granted them kindness, which follows patience. Then hearts filled with goodness bless those around us; and faithfulness says that, out of obedience to God's command, we are choosing to love, and thereby we become faithful to God. Our spirits become gentle, and self-control leads the way — after all, self-control is what it took to choose to love and to be filled with joy and peace in the first place. And God says there is no law against such things. Use them often, so that your heart will be filled with love, joy, and peace. Use them with zeal, because they never wear out and never go out of style. Use them, because it takes a lot more love, a lot more strength, a lot more character and desire to love God and to walk filled with the Spirit of God than to be hateful, demanding, critical, judgmental, a my-way-or-the-highway type of person. It is easy to hate; everyone is doing it. It is easy to be filled with pride and arrogance and abuse those around us. Let us choose to live in obedience to the only true God by asking Him to help us to learn to love the way He does. God will honor that request with a huge smile and a "well done, my good and faithful servant." It is love epitomized! Christianity is not for the faint of heart.

8

The Mystery of Forgiveness

I really believe that unforgiveness is the greatest problem we face in the church today. We say we forgive, but our actions and the thoughts running amuck in our minds tell a different story. What we do not realize is that failure to forgive the way God commands us leaves us sick, diseased, and filled with anxiety. God spoke this truth to me while I was dwelling on the mystery of forgiveness. God said there is no forgiveness without forgiveness. "But if you do not forgive men their sins, your Father will not forgive your sins" (Matthew 6:15) NIV. God teaches us that He will not forgive us unless we forgive others. Therein lies the mystery. The first thing we need to understand about forgiveness is that it is for us. Forgiveness is not for the person that has hurt, abused, or used us. When we forgive, we are set free! Forgiveness sets *me* free, not the person who hurt me — they still have to deal with the Most High God. When we choose to forgive others for what they have done to us, we honor God. It also helps us to be set free from bitterness, resentment, hate, and a host of illnesses. An unforgiving spirit makes us sick, filling us with disease, fear, worry, dread, and anxiousness. Deciding not to forgive is opting to suffer over and over again. When we choose not to forgive others, God chooses not to forgive us. Forgiveness can only be obtained through forgiveness.

Read what the Bible says in the following verses. "Whenever you stand praying, forgive, if you have anything against anyone, so that your Father who is in heaven will also forgive you your transgressions. But if you do not forgive, neither will your Father who is in heaven forgive your transgressions" (Mark 11:25-26). Is that clear enough? If we don't forgive, we are not forgiven! This means if we hold grudges, harbor jealousy in our hearts, or have bitterness toward anyone, we are living in sin. In fact, the Bible teaches us that God forgives us the same way we forgive others. I need to remember this when I decide I am going to hold on to bitterness, resentment, and hate because I refuse to forgive completely. I say I have forgiven a person; but if I continue to dwell on what they did and what I would like to do or say in order to repay them for what they did, that is not forgiveness. True forgiveness does not keep a record of wrongs. True forgiveness does not dwell on the past. True forgiveness begins with love and has the desire to be reconciled. This is why forgiveness is divine. I cannot forgive the way God expects me to without His power working in and through me. I need God's help, and I need to ask for it. Sometimes what God expects is impossible for us in our own power. God wants us to ask for His power, which can set us free from the torment brought on through unforgiveness.

In truth, only God can help us forgive in this way. We have to depend on Him to set us free from the hurt and pain by walking with Him, choosing obedience, and asking Him to help us be obedient. Once we choose this path, God will begin to deliver us. We become more than conquerors, because we are relying on the power of His Holy Spirit. Hurt and pain begin to lose their hold on us. In a relationship with God, we can ask for help on a moment-by-moment basis. Life begins to take on new meaning, and we discover that what we once thought was impossible is becoming reality — we are being set free. As we go through each day, we may have to call on God numerous times because our minds want to return to the scene of the crime and replay things over and over again. This will only overwhelm us, imprison us, even destroy us. At times it is our enemy, the devil, reminding us, because he knows so well how to get our minds off of the holy and onto memories that can start all these bad feelings once again. At other times it is our flesh which, deep down, wants revenge and retaliation, a way to get even, thinking this will somehow alleviate our pain. The truth and the mystery are that only God can heal us from the past; but we must be willing to forgive completely, which is only possible through His power. It is God's power that can deliver us from a life of torment into a life of power and love.

> Pray, then, in this way: 'Our Father who is in heaven, hallowed be Your name. Your kingdom come. Your will be done, on earth as it is in heaven. Give us this day our daily bread. And forgive us our debts, as we also have forgiven our debtors. And do not lead us into temptation, but deliver us from evil. For Yours is the kingdom and the power and the glory forever. Amen.' For if you forgive others for their transgressions, your heavenly Father will also forgive you. But if you do not forgive others, then your Father will not forgive your transgressions (Matthew 6:9-15).

Debts, iniquity, transgressions, and sins are all words that mean things done wrong; they are just used differently depending on the Bible translation you are studying. Debts or transgressions are things we continue to do even after being set free from a specific act of wrongdoing, or things we continue to do even though we know they are wrong. Iniquity is better translated "wickedness," and you will be surprised what God considers wicked — things like hate, jealously, envy, gossip, and the list goes on. Sin is what we do every day until we learn to walk filled with the Spirit. Sin is doing my own thing my own way, regardless of what God wants me to do or is trying to teach me. All these negative thoughts and actions border on unbelief.

Stand by Faith Believing in God

If we truly believed in God and that He is present with us at all times, some of our negative thoughts and actions would fall by the wayside immediately. The Bible teaches us that we are forgiven in the same way we forgive. Read it again: forgive us our sins as we forgive those who against us. In our present day language, we are asking God to forgive us the same way we forgive others. Do we really want to be forgiven the same way we forgive others? Do we forgive but choose not to be reconciled? I wonder how life would be if God chose not to be reconciled to us. Do we forgive but still hold a grudge and have hate in our hearts? What if God chose to hold a grudge against me due to my level of forgiveness? I really need to be more thorough in my forgiveness; I still tend to hold grudges and hate and become jealous and envious. I hold on to these negative qualities because I do not think the person who hurt me is being punished enough. How much will I have to endure for choosing unforgiveness? When I choose to hold bitterness in my heart and constantly dwell on the past, then my past becomes my god, and I have put myself into a prison of my own making. My past drains me of life and energy, causing great anxiety.

I could choose to focus on things above, things that refresh me, things that God would want me to give attention to. I could choose to mediate on God's Word or memorize a portion of the Scriptures that really speaks to me. I could think about heaven or the beauty that surrounds me. I could choose to think about things that are uplifting or even thought provoking, like what I read or studied in my time alone with God. Instead, I choose to be bound by and worship my past. God wants to help me overcome the prison I have built that is making my heart black. And because of the truths found in His Word, He is succeeding. I was constantly being tormented by my past because I chose to dwell on things done to me by people I loved and trusted. Now I know the truth, and I want to be forgiven totally, so I know that I need to forgive others totally. I also know that I cannot do this under my own power, so I continue to ask God to help me forgive the way He wants me to forgive. Each time unforgiving thoughts return, I will remind myself that I have forgiven and ask God to give me what I need to continue to forgive. God has also been teaching me that when I forgive someone, I am choosing to have compassion on them and to have a heart filled with mercy and grace. Mercy and grace move me to pray for blessings on those who have hurt me. I pray for their salvation and ask God to draw this person or persons closer to Him. In turn, God is pouring out His compassion on me, being merciful to me and His grace is mine daily. Hallelujah!

I have portions of the Scriptures written on flash cards to help me memorize and help me to dwell on God and His Word instead of on negative things. "Your word I have treasured in my heart, that I may not sin against You" (Psalm 119:11). God is also teaching me about forgiving self. I need to forgive myself and not allow my past to be a hindrance. God is teaching me how arrogant it is to hold on to my past. When I say I cannot do something, God tells me "I can do all things through Him who strengthens me" (Philippians 4:13). I think I cannot do this or that, but God says I can do all things through His power. When I do not choose what is right and good, the truth is not that I can't, but that I won't. How arrogant is it for me to choose not to forgive when God does? The Bible teaches that God chooses to forgive completely and even forget. If God can forgive me, then what does that say when I choose not to forgive myself or others? How arrogant am I, if the God of the universe chooses to forgive me and yet I choose not to forgive myself or others? Read what Jesus is saying here:

> Then Peter came and said to Him, "Lord, how often shall my brother sin against me and I forgive him? Up to seven times?" Jesus said to him, "I do not say to you, up to seven times, but up to seventy times seven. For this reason the kingdom of heaven may be compared to a king who wished to settle accounts with his slaves. When he had begun to settle them, one who owed him ten thousand talents was brought to him. But since he did not have the means to repay, his lord commanded him to be sold, along with his wife and children and all that he had, and repayment to be made. So the slave fell to the ground and prostrated himself before him, saying, 'Have patience with me and I will repay you everything.' And the lord of that slave felt compassion and released him and forgave him the debt. But that slave went out and found one of his fellow slaves who owed him a hundred denarii; and he seized him and began to choke him, saying, 'Pay back what you owe.' So his

fellow slave fell to the ground and began to plead with him, saying, 'Have patience with me and I will repay you.' But he was unwilling and went and threw him in prison until he should pay back what was owed. So when his fellow slaves saw what had happened, they were deeply grieved and came and reported to their lord all that had happened. Then summoning him, his lord said to him, 'You wicked slave, I forgave you all that debt because you pleaded with me. 'Should you not also have had mercy on your fellow slave, in the same way that I had mercy on you?' And his lord, moved with anger, handed him over to the torturers until he should repay all that was owed him. My heavenly Father will also do the same to you, if each of you does not forgive his brother from your heart" (Matthew 18:21-35).

When we choose not to forgive we are tormented by our past. Check it out: "And his lord, moved with anger, handed him over to the torturers." That is what we do when we focus on our past, choosing to dwell on the hurt and pain instead of on the One who can heal our pain. Anything we focus on continually, any wrong act we do that takes away from worshipping the one true God is an idol. When we spend large amounts of time and energy dwelling on our past, it becomes detrimental to our physical, mental, and emotional health. Anxiety begins to rule our lives and we spiral downward into depression. What we need to realize is that we are choosing to dwell on the past. Make no mistake, the only ones helping us in this endeavor are dark powers of evil. When we are overwhelmed by something and we let it control our thought lives, making us miserable and tormented, we are sinning against God. We have become wicked servants. Rather, this is what God would have us to do: "Whatever is true, whatever is honorable, whatever is right, whatever is pure, whatever is lovely, whatever is of good repute, if there is any excellence and if anything worthy of praise, dwell on these things" (Philippians 4:8).

How much easier would life be if we decided to think only positive, uplifting thoughts? What if we chose to focus on God, Jesus, heaven, or those in our lives that bring us joy? How much easier and enjoyable would life be if we chose to look for good in every situation? What if we chose to forgive, which frees us, instead of choosing to hold grudges or think up ways of paying back those who have hurt us? What if we chose to stop feeling sorry for ourselves? We need to turn from our past and look to God, who is able to help us forgive and move on. Being able to forgive completely and be reconciled is something that can only be done by God's power working in and through us. It is part of the higher calling of God that Paul talks about. "Brethren, I do not regard myself as having laid hold of it yet; but one thing I do: forgetting what lies behind and reaching forward to what lies ahead, I press on toward the goal for the prize of the upward call of God in Christ Jesus" (Philippians 3:13-14). Paul says he has yet to live in perfect obedience to God; but in the process of striving to live a godly life, he is doing what is most necessary to keep him in the battle. Paul does not want to give the devil a foothold and lose ground where God has already given him deliverance. God wants to set us free, but we want to hold on to the past, wrongly believing that it gives us power over whoever has hurt us. This is just the opposite of what God wants for us — He wants us to attempt the impossible, because He knows we will have to come to Him and ask for His help. That is exactly where God wants to be: right in the middle of our suffering, giving us the strength, power, and perseverance to overcome.

Bless those who persecute you; bless and do not curse. Rejoice with those who rejoice, and weep with those who weep. Be of the same mind toward one another; do not be haughty in mind, but associate with the lowly. Do not be wise in your own estimation. Never pay back evil for evil to anyone. Respect what is right in the sight of all men. If possible, so far as it depends on you, be at peace with all men. Never take your own revenge, beloved, but leave room for the wrath of God, for is written, 'Vengeance is Mine, I will repay,' says the Lord, 'But if your enemy is hungry, feed him, and if he is thirsty, give him a drink; for in so doing you will heap burning coals on his head.' Do not be overcome by evil, but overcome evil with good (Romans 12:14-21).

Are we going to trust in God or trust in ourselves? Live in our own self-created misery, or ask God to help us be more than conquerors? If we love God and we are living out our calling, He will make good things come of all the bad. All of us have had to endure things that were not fair, some even downright evil — things that leave us asking God "Why?" But when we choose to forgive and trust Him to do a perfect work in all the pain we have endured, God promises to bring good things that will bless us. God wants to work wonderful miracles in our lives; but if we choose not to obey Him, we will suffer and be tormented. God blesses obedience. It is only natural to hate, to be vengeful, to be critical, judgmental, overbearing, and hateful. We want vengeance! But God says that vengeance is His. When we try to get our own form of vengeance, we are standing in God's place, saying we know better than God how to take care of those who have done us wrong. We are choosing to spurn the sovereignty of God. How arrogant!

We need to remember that God says that we are judged in the same way we judge. "Do not judge so that you will not be judged. For in the way you judge, you will be judged; and by your standard of measure, it will be measured to you" (Matthew 7:1-2). It takes great character and a deep, abiding love for God to choose His way of forgiveness, love, and reconciliation; and without choosing to call on His power we will never overcome the past. When we ask God to help us to forgive, help us to love, help us to seek peace in every relationship, God hears these requests and will bless us beyond our wildest dreams for choosing to obey, for choosing to please Him. That is worship! Choosing to please God says, "I love you, God, and I want to live my life according to your plans for me." And God says, "Things which eye has not seen and ear has not heard, and which have not entered the heart of man, all that God has prepared for those who love Him" (1 Corinthians 2:9). We cannot even imagine what God has prepared for us now, in the future, and in heaven. We cannot even imagine what God wants to do in our hearts if we will only trust Him. Here again is a choice that God puts before us. Will we choose obedience, or will we try to fix ourselves in our own power and be imprisoned again? I desire to dwell on things that are beautiful. I want the Words of Christ to dwell in me. I know it is much easier to hate than to love, easier to focus on the past instead of living in the present with bright hope for the future. Again, living in obedience to God is not for the faint of heart. It is easy to do what comes naturally — weak-willed people do it every day. God wants us to depend on His power, to live a supernatural life filled by His Spirit. Our focus needs to be on the high calling of God on our lives.

> So, as those who have been chosen of God, holy and
> beloved, put on a heart of compassion, kindness,
> humility, gentleness and patience; bearing with one

another, and forgiving each other, whoever has a complaint against anyone; just as the Lord forgave you, so also should you. Beyond all these things put on love, which is the perfect bond of unity. Let the peace of Christ rule in your hearts, to which indeed you were called in one body; and be thankful. Let the word of Christ richly dwell within you, with all wisdom teaching and admonishing one another with psalms and hymns and spiritual songs, singing with thankfulness in your hearts to God. Whatever you do in word or deed, do all in the name of the Lord Jesus, giving thanks through Him to God the Father (Colossians 3:12-17).

This is the only way we will move from the past and live for God from now until forever. And when we think that we are not as bad as some people or have not done things like those we have complaints against, let us be reminded that this is pride, and pride is sin. Our enemy, the devil, was thrown out of heaven because of pride. The Bible says, "All have sinned and fall short of the glory of God" (Romans 3:23). "For the wages of sin is death, but the free gift of God is eternal life in Christ Jesus our Lord" (Romans 6:23). "As it is written, 'There is none righteous, not even one" Romans 3:10). When we compare our level of sin to others, we are trying to be justified by the law; and no one can be made righteous by the law, only by faith.

Two men went up into the temple to pray, one a Pharisee and the other a tax collector. The Pharisee stood and was praying this to himself: 'God, I thank You that I am not like other people: swindlers, unjust, adulterers, or even like this tax collector. I fast twice a week; I pay tithes of all that I get.' But the tax collector, standing some distance away, was even unwilling to lift up his eyes to heaven, but was beating his breast, saying, 'God, be merciful to me, the sinner!' I tell you, this man went to his house justified rather than the other; for everyone who exalts himself will be humbled, but he who humbles himself will be exalted (Luke 18:10-14).

Have you ever made a comment like this? "I am not as bad as . . . I have never done . . ." I challenge you to think about those who have been deeply hurt by your words. Think about those you do not like. Think about how proud one becomes believing in oneself and one's own power and remember "*all have sinned*". According to God, hate is murder. I say I have never committed adultery, and then I think about how lust used to rule my life. Jesus says that when I look upon a woman with lust in my heart, I have committed adultery. If the truth be known, I am a sinner of sinners, not unlike some of the worst people in all of Scripture. So, when I come before God in prayer I plead, "God, be merciful to me, the sinner." Christianity is not for the faint of heart.

9

God Commands Us to Love

The Bible is the best way to gain real knowledge of who God is and to learn the heart of God. As I have written earlier, God's heart is that you choose to love Him and to love others. The Bible tells us that God is love. "Beloved, let us love one another, for love is from God; and everyone who loves is born of God and knows God. The one who does not love does not know God, for God is love" (1 John 4:7-8). God commands us to love; therefore, love is a choice, not a feeling. That feeling you get when you meet someone is infatuation. People do not fall in and out of love; we choose whether we will love someone or not. I hear people talk about falling out of love with their spouses, but the truth is that they have chosen not to love them anymore for whatever reason. There is no longer any fellowship between the two, because their hearts are focused on the negative aspects of their relationship, things done wrong, or other people; and they no longer spend time together growing in a give-and-take relationship. One or both choose not to be committed to each other any longer. If love was natural, then God would not have had to command us to love. Jesus put it this way when He tells us the greatest commandment in the Scriptures:

The foremost is, 'Hear, O Israel! The Lord our God is
one Lord; and you shall love the Lord your God with
all your heart, and with all your soul, and with all
your mind, and with all your strength.' The second is
this, 'You shall love your neighbor as yourself.' There
is no other commandment greater than these (Mark
12:29-31).

To love — that is what God wants of us. When we choose
love, we are choosing to please God. Choosing love pleases God,
because loving Him is believing in Him. Loving each other
shows our obedience to Him. It can be difficult, but choosing to
love is living in obedience to God's commands, and God blesses
obedience.

Let us go back to infatuation for a minute. Infatuation is an
intense but a very short lived irrational passion for somebody.
Short lived — that is where the "falling out" comes in. People fall
out of love because they were never in love to begin with — they
were enamored by, infatuated with, in lust. Once the newness
wore off, instead of choosing to love, they chose to leave. Loving
is not easy. Think about wedding vows. To love, honor, and
cherish, in sickness and in health, for richer or for poorer, for
better or worse. It is a shame that we do not put more thought
into these vows before we say, "I do." Seriously, when the
newness wears off, we do not even think about the commitment
we made. How sad that it is nothing to be married several times
in a lifetime. Even adultery is no longer committing adultery;
no, no, it's much nicer now, because we call it "having an affair."
What a shame. How many lives are shattered by divorce? We
need to realize that it is not just the spouse who is hurt by
such a terrible, selfish act. It hurts your parents, who have
chosen to love your spouse; your in-laws, who have chosen to
love you; and the children suffer the most. The children, who

love their mothers and fathers with an unconditional love are left wondering, "What did we do?" Children will often believe they said or did something wrong to cause this calamity — even after we try to tell them it is nothing they have done it is just that we do not love each other anymore. Now, how is a child supposed to understand that? Children love their parents unconditionally, and children believe that there is nothing their mom or dad cannot do. I wonder if the children who are in the midst of this are thinking, "If my mom and dad do not love each other anymore, are they going to stop loving me?" How will a child ever understand the concept of unconditional love if their mothers and fathers cannot demonstrate this type of love for each other?

This is why God hates divorce. It destroys families. I can say this since I have firsthand knowledge of what divorce does to families, being divorced and from a broken home. In truth, what we should say is that we are choosing not to love our spouses anymore because it is hard work — not to mention how hard it is to love me, because I am selfish, spoiled, and cannot be pleased because I want what I want and I want it now. People say that the grass is always greener on the other side. I heard a pastor say on more than one occasion that the grass is greener where you water it. When I choose to love someone, I spend time getting to know them. If I want to demonstrate my love for my wife, I look for opportunities to make her feel special. I do things that I know she likes, and I try not to do things I know she does not like. If we have a disagreement, I will realize that I do not have to be right all the time. I work at pleasing my wife not because of what she does or does not do but because I have made a commitment to her — a commitment to love, honor, and cherish, for richer or for poorer, in sickness and in health, for better or worse. This means that there is nothing she can do or say that can keep me from choosing to love her. That is the meaning of unconditional love, and we cannot love like this apart from the Holy Spirit of God. If you do not know God, if you do not have a personal, intimate relationship with God, you cannot love with this type of love. Even when we are filled with the Spirit of God and trying to live in a way that pleases God there will be times when we fail.

When our spouses fall into some type of an addiction, like alcohol, drugs, or pornography, the last thing they need is for us leave them. They are sick and need us to love unconditionally, pray for them, and try to help them. When we fail each other, we need the other to go above and beyond their strength and power and ask God to help them to love us unconditionally. This is part of that higher calling God gives us. He can help us, sustain us, and work miracles in our lives if we will look to Him for help in times like this. He is our healer; and when we run away from problems instead of facing them and asking God for help, our faith wanes. What we are saying is that our problem is more than God can handle when in truth it is our faith in Him which is lacking.

Dedication, Commitment, Perseverance

If you want to live life to the fullest, then love. If you really want to be happy, to exude joy, and to have peace fill your heart, then love — love with all your heart. Let love be what flavors your words, actions, and thoughts. Ask God to fill your heart with love — to help you to love Him with all your heart, soul, mind, and strength. It is the way God tells us He wants to be loved. Then, and only then, will we be able to love people with the type of love God wants us to demonstrate. Learning to love is a process, and it moves us from being selfish to giving ourselves away. When we ask God to help us love Him, He will also help us to love each other.

I have been the most selfish person in the world. I know what lust looks and sounds like; I know what it is to be self-centered, using people for my pleasure regardless of their wants and desires. I know what it feels like to be loved and cast aside as well as to love and cast another aside. This is not love, it's abuse. It is using and abusing then moving on to get my needs met. I have been there, I have done that; and I have asked God for forgiveness over and over again, even though the Bible teaches me that God forgave me the first time I confessed these actions. I pray and ask God to help me so that I can love in a way that brings glory to God. I ask Him to help me love Him with all my heart, soul, mind and strength. God has been teaching me how to love and I have been slow about learning the right way. I am getting better, but trying to change after years of living a self-centered life is a struggle. Change is difficult and old habits die hard, but any good thing takes hard work, commitment, and dedication.

If you want a youthful body and appearance, you will have to exercise and eat right. It is the only way. If you want knowledge, you will have to read, study, and research. If there is anything you want to be good at, it will take time and effort. Nothing good comes easily; without dedication, commitment, study, and practice, you will not reach your goal. It is difficult to learn to play an instrument; it takes devotion to study and practice to achieve greatness. It is the same way with any sport — you must be committed to doing everything necessary to reach your goal. How many people love to run? Most sports require miles and miles of running in order to be fit to play. If you are going to be any good, you must be physically fit. There are no shortcuts. It takes hard work, dedication, perseverance, pushing yourself to the limit and beyond. If you want to be knowledgeable about a subject, you must read, retain what you read, study, investigate, and research to achieve your goal. Look how long it takes to be a great doctor — years of study, years of practice, and the learning never ends. It is the same way with a good lawyer, nurse, accountant, teacher, plumber, mechanic, or carpenter. You will not be the best unless you dedicate your life to it. If there is no commitment, there is only mediocrity. Since we know this, how much time and effort should we give toward loving others? How much time, dedication, perseverance, commitment, and devotion should we give to being the best parent, the best spouse, the best sibling, the best child, the best friend?

God commands us to love because love is a choice and not a feeling. We choose to love or not to love. It is not about falling in and out of love, it is about choosing love. God is love, and therefore the author of love, and He teaches us what unconditional love looks and acts like — quick to forgive and ready to encourage, that gives until it hurts and then gives some more. Love chooses never to give up — runs to you, falls on you, cries with you, and prays for you until there is nothing else to give and then . . . and then God steps in and pours Himself out on us.

> What then shall we say to these things? If God is for us, who is against us? He who did not spare His own Son, but delivered Him over for us all, how will He not also with Him freely give us all things? Who will bring a charge against God's elect? God is the one who justifies; who is the one who condemns? Christ Jesus is He who died, yes, rather who was raised, who is at the right hand of God, who also intercedes for

us. Who will separate us from the love of Christ? Will tribulation, or distress, or persecution, or famine, or nakedness, or peril, or sword? Just as it is written, 'For Your sake we are being put to death all day long; we were considered as sheep to be slaughtered.' But in all these things we overwhelmingly conquer through Him who loved us. For I am convinced that neither death, nor life, nor angels, nor principalities, nor things present, nor things to come, nor powers, nor height, nor depth, nor any other created thing, will be able to separate us from the love of God, which is in Christ Jesus our Lord (Romans 8:31-39).

It is only by the love God gives that you will be able to love the unlovable and forgive those who have hurt you. It is through love that you will find life truly amazing and exciting. You will wake up every day desiring to impact the lives of those around you with a love that strengthens, encourages, builds relationships, and never gives up. We must commit to love in order to achieve the highest of all goals. I wonder what that looks like. What does love look and feel like when someone chooses to be committed to love?

Love is patient, love is kind. It does not envy, it does not boast, it is not proud. It does not dishonor others, it is not self-seeking, it is not easily angered, it keeps no record of wrongs. Love does not delight in evil but rejoices with the truth. It always protects, always trusts, always hopes, always perseveres (1 Corinthians 13:4-7 NIV).

The Greatest is Love

Wow — how can I ever hope to love like this? I know it is impossible without God's power at work in my life. And even with God's power, sometimes I must choose moment by moment to love. I must choose love. Love is what overcomes hate and removes bitterness and resentment. Love will help you overcome being critical, judgmental, and overbearing — which is arrogance, by the way. It is easy and even natural to hate; it is easy to put people down so that we can feel good about ourselves. It is easy to point the finger and blame others for the way we are. But the truth is that we are the way we are because we choose to be that way. No one has the power to make us act a certain way unless we give it to them. No one has the power to make us hate, put down, or condescend — we have to choose how we respond to people. And if we use the past as an excuse, then our past is our god. The Bible says, "I can do all things through Him who strengthens me" (Philippians 4:13) and "But in all these things we overwhelmingly conquer through Him who loved us" (Romans 8:37). When we say we can't, we make God (who says we can) to be a liar! We can do all things! Read the book *Tortured for Christ* by Richard Wurmbrand, the founder of Voice of the Martyrs. These men, who had terrible atrocities committed against them daily for many years, learned they could choose to love their torturers. Wurmbrand says that he cannot even tell of some of the things done to them because of the nightmares they bring when reliving them. His book goes on to tell the story of some of what they endured and how they overcame the daily torture by choosing to love their enemies. It is truly an amazing story.

We all have a choice as to how we respond to wrongs committed against us no matter how terrible. We can choose to hate, to want to see the other person punished, or we can choose love. Remember, God blesses obedience. Hate will take us down a road of deep suffering and torment. Hate makes the body, heart, soul, and mind sick and can even kill us. Again, hate makes us critical, overbearing, judgmental and invites bitterness and resentment to rule our lives. Hate equals unforgiveness. Choosing not to forgive is hate, and it colors our world black. We become diseased, mentally, physically, emotionally, and spiritually.

Love, on the other hand, is supernatural. You cannot truly love without the love of God ruling your heart. Please do not miss that last statement. Love is supernatural, and only the love that God has demonstrated towards us will overcome hate. I thought I loved when I was without God; but I have since discovered that my love was pathetic, selfish and about what I could get from people. I will love someone as long as they do what I like, do what I say, and be like I want them to be. And when they stop adoring me or start talking ill of me or doing things I do not like, then I am gone. There is no real commitment.

Commitment and love go hand in hand. You cannot truly love someone if you are not committed to them. Commitment says, "I choose love. No matter how difficult life becomes, I want to honor God." If we were truly committed, divorce would not be so rampant, and broken families would not be the norm. Children would honor their parents because of love, and parents would love their children. There would not be such a great need for nursing homes, because children would want to take care of ailing parents no matter what the cost. And even if they had to put their parents in nursing homes, they would visit several times a week instead of every once in a great while or never. There would be no need for orphanages, because so many families would want to take in those children who had lost their parents. We would not spend our lives working in order to have more things. We would want to work less and live with less in order to enjoy each other. We would find things that we could do together and would find pleasure in our differences. We would laugh together, love together, and even cry and hurt together. We would realize that true love requires suffering, sometimes at the hands of those we love the most. It takes great perseverance and commitment to pick up our cross daily and choose to follow Jesus. Suffering is part of life, and that is what hones us to be the disciples that God is calling us to be. Paul reminds us about our suffering when he says, "for I consider that the sufferings of this present time are not worthy to be compared with the glory that is to be revealed to us" (Romans 8:18).

The pursuit of happiness is not found in things but by impacting each other's lives with our talents, abilities, gifts — and, yes, even our flaws, failures, mistakes, and differences of personality. We all do things that are wrong, that hurt, and that can even greatly mar lives. If it was not for forgiveness, we would not have any hope. But there is hope because of God. Each day is a new beginning. "The Lord's lovingkindnesses indeed never cease, for His compassions never fail. They are new every morning; great is Your faithfulness. 'The Lord is my portion,' says my soul, 'therefore I have hope in Him.' The Lord is good to those who wait for Him, to the person who seeks Him" (Lamentations 3:22-25). So we start each day anew impacting those around us with love. We choose love and forgiveness, just as the Lord chooses to deal with us through love and forgiveness. We should begin each day asking God to fill us with His Spirit, to help us do what is pleasing in His sight in everything we say and do and think. This is what it means to be in a personal, intimate relationship with God and to walk filled with His Spirit. True love says, "I forgive you, even without you asking for forgiveness." If someone ever comes to me to ask for forgiveness, I hope I have already forgiven them. True love says, "I care about you and the things you care about."

> Do nothing from selfishness or empty conceit, but with humility of mind regard one another as more important than yourselves; do not merely look out for your own personal interests, but also for the interests of others. Have this attitude in yourselves which was also in Christ Jesus (Philippians 2:3-5).

God commands us to love and to choose forgiveness. It is what God has done through Jesus Christ. God sent Jesus to pay for the sins of the world, which He did through His death on the cross. Jesus obeyed God, left heaven and was born a man, walked a sinless life, then was crucified and died on a cross so that our wrongdoings (sin) could be forgiven. Now God tells us to pick up our crosses daily and follow His example: an example of suffering, of denying self, and of living a life that is pleasing to God. If we do, our lives will be filled with blessings. God blesses obedience. Look at where Jesus is now: since Jesus chose to obey God, He is now at God's right hand with all authority and power.

> Have this attitude in yourselves which was also in Christ Jesus, who, although He existed in the form of God, did not regard equality with God a thing to be grasped, but emptied Himself, taking the form of a bond-servant, and being made in the likeness of men. Being found in appearance as a man, He humbled Himself by becoming obedient to the point

of death, even death on a cross. For this reason also, God highly exalted Him, and bestowed on Him the name which is above every name, so that at the name of Jesus every knee will bow, of those who are in heaven and on earth and under the earth, and that every tongue will confess that Jesus Christ is Lord, to the glory of God the Father (Philippians 2:5-11).

All Will Bow

Read all of Philippians chapter 2 and see for yourself. We will either bow now, while we still have life and a choice, or we will bow when we die and stand before God. When we die and stand in God's presence, seeing firsthand how awesome He is and how incredible it is to be in His presence, and then realize that since we did not choose God while we were still living, we do not get to live in His presence for eternity. If we choose to reject God, not believe in Him, and tell Him we do not need Him, then God will not make us spend eternity with Him. It is the choice every person gets to make. To live with God or without God for eternity — it is your choice.

Try to imagine what it is going to be like the first time we see God. We die, we are carried by our angels into heaven, and we are brought to the throne room — and there we see God, with Jesus sitting at His right hand. How long will we gaze upon the Most High God before we are able to tear our gazes away from such an awesome sight and go exploring heaven? We will be standing there, filled with awe, taking in the beauty of the Lord of lords and the King of kings. Dumbfounded, we will stand looking at the Creator and Sustainer of all of heaven and earth. If we have lived by faith in the One True God, He will welcome us into heaven. And can you even imagine what

His voice must sound like? The One who has sustained heaven and earth since the beginning of time; our Creator, the One who allows us every breath we take and every move we make; the Almighty God, who stood with us in our times of joy and happiness, who carried us in our times of deepest sorrow and grief, and who loved us in our worst sin, will be welcoming us to an eternity with Him.

For the first time, we will get to see the Omnipotent, Omniscient, Omnipresent God face to face, and the sight of Him will no doubt take our breath away — the sovereign Lord, indescribable in His magnificence, His grandeur, His awesome beauty, so we stand there captivated by God — a vision so spectacular, so incredible, so stunning that we cannot bear to look away. God will be the most incredible sight we have ever encountered, and then the wonderful realization will hit us that we get to spend an eternity with Him. Time will be no more and we can stand there taking in the incredible sight of God for as long as our hearts desire. We are there to stay. We get to be there because we decided to trust God, confessing Jesus with our mouths and believing in our hearts that God has raised Jesus from the dead. We chose to be obedient, to put our faith in Jesus Christ and His redeeming work on the cross. When God called our names, we said, "Here I am, Lord," and began a walk of faith, believing that no matter what life held in store for us, God was going to get us home to be with Him forever.

No matter how many times I failed no matter what I did or did not do, I placed my faith in Jesus Christ. Period! I did nothing to earn heaven; I put my faith in God knowing that Jesus died to pay for my every sin and my every failure, and now I am trusting God to bring me all the way home. Going to church did not earn me a place in heaven. Being a good person did not earn me a place in heaven, and doing good things did not earn me a place in heaven. "For by grace you have been saved through faith; and that not of yourselves, it is the gift of God; not as a result of works" (Ephesians 2:8-9). It was simply because of the grace of God that I chose faith in Jesus Christ, and now God will allow me to enter His presence and be with Him for eternity. Listen to what Jesus says: "I am the way, and the truth, and the life; no one comes to the Father but through Me" (John 14:6). No one comes to God the Father except through Jesus Christ. Listen again to what Paul tells us: "There is salvation in no one else; for there is no other name under heaven that has been given among men by which we must be saved" (Acts 4:12). That name is the name of Jesus. It is His finished work on the cross which provides us a way to be made right with God. When we believe, He will count it as righteousness. Just by believing God, we become righteous. Paul reminds us of this: "With the heart a person believes, resulting in righteousness, and with the mouth he confesses, resulting in salvation" (Romans 10:10). Faith is the victory that overcomes the world.

> Whoever believes that Jesus is the Christ is born of God, and whoever loves the Father loves the child born of Him. By this we know that we love the children of God, when we love God and observe His commandments. For this is the love of God, that we keep His commandments; and His commandments are not burdensome. For whatever is born of God overcomes the world; and this is the victory that has overcome the world—our faith. Who is the one who overcomes the world, but he who believes that Jesus is the Son of God? (1 John 5:1-5)

All Will Know That He is God

I want to make something very clear here. Every living soul will get to stand at the throne of God and see the most awesome, magnificent, and wonder-filled sight you will ever witness. When you find yourself standing before God, overwhelmed by His presence, enthralled by what you see, you will confess with your mouth that Jesus Christ is Lord, to the glory of God the Father. There will be no doubt that you have known God because you have walked through life with Him as your Savior and Lord. But if you have denied God and never asked Him to be part of your life, you will still stand before God and will know without a doubt that He is God. You will confess that He is God and that Jesus Christ is Lord; and as you stand before Him, confessing Him as God and being overwhelmed by everything around you — the sights you have never before witnessed, the sounds you have never heard, the smell and the feel of heaven — then you will realize that you do not get to stay.

Remember the Scripture I quoted earlier from Philippians 2:10-11? In my own words that every knee is going to bow and every mouth will confess Jesus as Lord. You must either confess now, willingly, and then gain heaven, a relationship with God through Jesus Christ, eternal life, His power and presence in your life; or you will bow willingly before the judgment seat of Christ because you will have no doubt whose presence you are in; and then, because you rejected God throughout your life, God will honor your request. You will not spend eternity with God in heaven but in a terrible place absent from the presence of God. That is my definition of Hell. It is a dark place, because the light of Christ is not there. It is a lonely place, because the Spirit of God is not there. It is a place of torment that can be avoided by simply asking God to be a part of your life.

Remember, without faith it is impossible to please God. Faith can set you free. Simple faith brings life — abundant life — life like you have never imagined, because God the Father, God the Son, and God the Holy Spirit will show you the way home. "You will make known to me the path of life; In Your presence is fullness of joy; in Your right hand there are pleasures forever" (Psalm 16:11) God wants to walk with each one of us as we go through each day. He wants us to walk filled by His Holy Spirit. If we allow the Holy Spirit to fill us each day, if we walk in obedience to God, our lives will be filled with wonder and awe.

So many people reject God because of Christians they know. The truth is that even as Christians we do things that are wrong. Christians are not perfect, just forgiven. I know good Christian people who struggle with addictions, broken marriages, foul mouths, and small faith. But God honors faith, no matter how small. According to God, even small faith can move mountains. The only difference between those who know God and those who do not is faith. Christians still have sin in their lives. But as Christians, when we grow in faith and begin to choose obedience to God's commands, we will sin less and less, complete perfection only being attainable in heaven. It is only when we give up this body of flesh and all our selfish desires that we will become perfect. When we are welcomed into heaven by Christ, we will no longer struggle with sin. This is a fact that must be faced. When we think we have attained sinless lives and begin to be proud of ourselves, therein lies our sin — pride! The only reason we have become better people is because we are continuing to learn to rely on the power of God's Holy Spirit and not on our own power. When we think, "Oh, I am not that bad, I have not done things like this person or that person, I am not as bad as he or she is," well, guess what — pride has entered our hearts and we are believing a lie. As faith grows, a Christian will choose to change his focus from his circumstances to Jesus. As we choose to pick up our crosses daily, we will choose to live lives that line up with the Bible. Paul begged us to live lives worthy of our calling because he understood the freedom obedience brings. It is not about giving things up but giving up the evil desires that are killing us. "For we must all appear before the judgment seat of Christ, so that each one may be recompensed for his deeds in the body, according to what he has done, whether good or bad" (2 Corinthians 5:10).

> Each man's work will become evident; for the day will show it because it is to be revealed with fire, and the fire itself will test the quality of each man's work. If any man's work which he has built on it remains, he will receive a reward. If any man's work is burned up, he will suffer loss; but he himself will be saved, yet so as through fire. Do you not know that you are a temple of God and that the Spirit of God dwells in you? (1 Corinthians 3:13-16).

We will all stand before God as our lives are reviewed; and for those of us who know God personally, His grace and mercy will be poured out because of what Jesus has done.

I know that I have caused much pain and hurt, mostly to those that I love deeply; and each day my past hinders my walk with God. Living life being ashamed is not what God wants. It is hard for me to put the past behind me and look forward to the high calling of God on my life. It is something that God is teaching me to do in spite of what others may do or think. The greatest news is that I have confessed my sins, and I want to be the person God has called me to be. God is at work in my life — changing me, teaching me, comforting me — and because

I make His Word part of my daily life, I am being discipled by God's Holy Spirit on a daily basis. "You will keep him in perfect peace, whose mind is stayed on You, because he trusts in You" (Isaiah 26:3 NKJV). If we will live by this verse, we will become more than conquerors! I want to spend the remaining time I have on this earth trying to help people succeed. I want to learn every day how to love God more and how to love people the way God intends; and I know I can only do this through God's power. "How blessed is he whose transgression is forgiven, whose sin is covered! How blessed is the man to whom the Lord does not impute iniquity, and in whose spirit there is no deceit!" (Psalm 32:1-2).

The Epitome of Love

Listen to what Jesus said while dying on the cross after walking on the earth for 33 years; after being spit on, slapped, slugged, beaten almost to death, laughed at, mocked, made fun of, and called a drunkard and a glutton; after being convicted on trumped-up charges and sentenced to die; and then after being nailed, naked, on a hard wooden cross an innocent man, listen to what Jesus says: "Father, forgive them; for they do not know what they are doing" (Luke 23:34). That is unconditional love! God chose to hang on a cross. He chose to allow these heinous crimes against Himself and to endure suffering in His own life. Finally, God chose forgiveness instead of hate. He did all this because of His great love for His creation, of which you and I are a part. The Bible says that "God demonstrates His own love toward us, in that while we were yet sinners, Christ died for us" (Romans 5:8). Christ died so that we can live, and He is our example. Jesus Christ died on a cross, was laid in a borrowed tomb, was raised to life three days later, and then sat down at the right hand of God, where He remains even now. Jesus — the same yesterday, today, and forever — has been given all authority in heaven and on earth; and He wants to show us the way to the Father. Not only does Jesus want to show us the way, but He has also given us His Holy Spirit to guide us, to direct us, and to fill us with His power.

This is the constant pursuit of a Holy God who is madly in love with His creation. God wants to teach us about His great love for each one of us; and this can only be done if we choose to be in relationship with Him. God will not force Himself on us, but not a day goes by in each of our lives that God is not calling us to Himself. What most of us do not know or understand is that this is what our hearts are longing for; this is the yearning that worldly things cannot satisfy. Not until we enter into personal and intimate relationship with God will our lives ever have a sense of purpose and direction. If you want your life to have meaning, if you want to make a difference in this world, begin by choosing to love God with all your heart, soul, mind, and strength. Start today — ask God to help you to love Him the way He wants to be loved and to help you to love people the way He wants you to love people. If you ask God to forgive you of your sins and help change you into the person He wants you to be, He will. Jesus died for your sins so you could say, "I believe in Jesus; I believe You are the Son of God; I believe You died and rose again; I believe You paid for my sins; and I believe You are here with me now." If you say this, believe it, and mean it, then God will save you, enter into a relationship with you, and pour out eternal blessings upon you. Just continue to say and believe these powerful truths for the rest of your life. Remember Romans 10:9-10? "If you confess with your mouth Jesus as Lord, and believe in your heart that God raised Him from the dead, you will be saved; for with the heart a person believes, resulting in righteousness, and with the mouth he confesses, resulting in salvation." Live your life believing this and seeking God through His Word and prayer, and He will continue to pour His grace out upon you and fill your life with peace and joy.

In any relationship there are things we like and things we do not like about the other person. It takes commitment, perseverance, a forgiving and forgetful heart, and a desire to keep our commitments in order to love unconditionally; and we cannot do it without the power of God's Holy Spirit. None of us have this power apart from a relationship with God. Once we enter into a relationship with Him, He will fill us with His Holy Spirit. Then, through His power, we will begin to learn to love. If we could love the way God intended without His power, then there would not be so many marriages ending in divorce. There would not be so many broken homes. People would not just live together without making the commitment of marriage. People fail daily to be committed, choosing instead to commit heinous crimes against one another — crimes like adultery, abandonment, sexual promiscuity, abuse (sexual, mental, emotional, and physical), murder, rape, and the list goes on. We lie, cheat, and steal, trying to fill a void within. We play video games, watch TV game shows or reality TV, trying to live our lives vicariously through the lives of others. We spend hours in competition, playing sports, on the computer, or texting on our cell phones, building relationships without any real depth. We become workaholics, alcoholics, addicted to drugs, sex, or food. Many of us are in search of things to bring fulfillment into our lives and to take up our time so we can forget our failures. We work ourselves to death, saying we want to give our children all the things we never had, while failing to give them what they need. What children really need is a relationship with their mother and father. Our children need love — they need boundaries, discipline, direction, and someone who will listen to them and help them as they try to figure out what life is all about. They need us to teach them about God and His great love for them. Instead, we seek to fulfill our own selfish desires, no matter who gets hurt and left behind in the process, believing that someone or something else has what we need in order to be complete. We fill our lives with things that drain us of life instead of giving fulfillment. We will continue down this path of self-destruction until we decide to become obedient to God. And all that God is asking us to do is to love. Again, it is what we are all searching for — only sometimes we believe our possessions can make us happy, or sex, drugs, or activities that dull our minds to the truth. All of us are searching for love that is unconditional, unchangeable, and accepts us for who we are, despite all of our fears and failures. This is the love that God offers us. I had never experienced love like God's until I began to seek Him, to learn what He does for me each day, and to know that His love for me is greater than any other. He does not stop loving me just because I do not love Him. Instead, He relentlessly pursues me until the day I die. God chooses to love me not because of what I have or have not done but because of who He is. "God is love" (1 John 4:16).

Jesus says, "the spirit is willing, but the flesh is weak" (Matthew 26:41b). God knows we are weak. However, as we grow in our faith and allow God's Spirit to work in and through us, we strive to please God by doing His will and not our own. We begin to experience God's love for us, and His love begins to transform us. When this happens, we find ourselves wanting to please God by loving people. We even choose to love those who are hard to love. Again, this is something divine, something supernatural that happens. God knows our hearts, and when our desire is to please Him, His power is released into our lives and we become different. We choose to love, we choose to forgive, and we choose to be obedient because our love for God is growing. When we begin to choose love, God will bless us for it. God blesses obedience. When we ask God to help us to love Him and to help us to love others, we begin to understand the mysteries of God. Christianity is not for the faint of heart.

10 ———————————

Faith = Belief + Trust

The Bible teaches us that we are saved by God's grace through faith. The word "saved" means we are rescued from eternal separation from God. We are released from death to eternal life with God in heaven. When our lives are done on this earth, God is preparing a place for each one who chooses to believe in Him and the finished work of Jesus Christ on the cross — the sinless life Jesus lived, His obedience to God through His death on the cross, His resurrection from the dead, and now His eternal reign at the right hand of the throne of God. God saves me when I choose to believe this reality. Now I need to choose to put my faith in God by believing and trusting. These are two elements to faith: trust and belief. These three things are needed in order to come into a relationship with God that is real and everlasting. "Trust in the Lord with all your heart and do not lean on your own understanding" (Proverbs 3:5). Without faith it is impossible to please God; and without believing in Him and trusting Him, faith is impossible. I know without a doubt that God has revealed Himself to us in great and mighty ways. Even while writing this sentence I cannot even come close to explaining the deep and secret things that God has revealed to us and how much more He has to share. The mystery begins with how God reveals Himself to us through the Scriptures, in nature, in our daily circumstances, and so many other ways.

Once you have chosen to believe, a change of heart takes place — one that cannot be explained. The moment you decide to believe, God gives you His Holy Spirit. "Now He who establishes us with you in Christ and anointed us is God, who also sealed us and gave us the Spirit in our hearts as a pledge" (2 Corinthians 1:21-22). The Spirit of the Living God dwells in us. How awesome! It is God's desire to be near to us, but He wants us to choose to be near to Him. "Draw near to God and He will draw near to you" (James 4:8a). God is not like us — He will not come barging in or force us to spend time with Him. However, He will continue to pursue us relentlessly until our dying day wanting to be a part of our lives even if we reject Him. I mean, come on — isn't your life messed up enough? Haven't you figured out yet that you do not have the power to fix it? God does! He wants to help us in our feeble attempts to live in a way that pleases Him. Faith pleases God! It is that simple and that complex. It is when we finally come to a place that we can say, "God, I know that I cannot do this, but I know without a doubt You can." Choosing to believe in God — that is faith. Taking God at His word and standing on His promises — that is trusting. And knowing God can do anything, knowing He has our best interest at heart — that is believing. It is true that God wants us to live life to the fullest. He wants our lives to be filled with expectation and adventure, better than any movie we have ever watched or any experience we have been through. God wants to lead us down a road filled with excitement and adventure, but we cannot travel that road without believing and trusting Him. God might want to do something in and through you that is so far above anything you have ever imagined; but without believing and trusting Him, it will never happen. "This I know, that God is for me. In God, whose word I praise, in the Lord, whose word I praise, in God I have put my trust, I shall not be afraid. What can man do to me?" (Psalm 56:9b-11). Trust is one of the hardest things to earn and the easiest to lose. With people it only takes one time of falling short to lose it; but it takes a lifetime to gain it back. Trust in God, who is never early and never late. Trust in God, who wants each one of us to succeed, even excel in life. At the center of the Bible, it says "It is better to take refuge in the Lord than to trust in man" (Psalm 118:8). I know placing that verse in the very center of God's Word was not by accident. God wants us to trust Him, He wants us to put our trust in Him. He has our best interest at heart. God wants us to succeed and, even more than that, to become more than conquerors.

Dying to Self

Trusting in man includes trusting in self — and I have already witnessed firsthand how well man can be trusted. Being self-reliant, self-confident or a self-made man are all lies of the enemy. It is God who made us and gave us life and breath; and when He chooses, we will breathe our last. If I say I am trusting in God, then I have placed my confidence in Him and in the finished work of Jesus Christ on the cross of Calvary. Because of this, the Bible tells me, "Therefore let us draw near with confidence to the throne of grace, so that we may receive mercy and find grace to help in time of need" (Hebrews 4:16). Living by faith means that I believe in God as the Almighty, the One True God, who has created heaven and earth and the seas and all that is in them. God not only created all things, but He continues to sustain all of life. God has not left us to ourselves unless we choose to live life without Him. Even then God still blesses our lives — God causes His sun to rise on both the evil and the good, and sends rain on both the righteous and on the unrighteous; and there is no denying that God gives us every breath we take. God wants us to choose to believe in Him, to place our trust in Him. Choosing to believe in God will bring blessings into our lives, because God rewards those who choose to believe. Faith is a combination of belief and trust, which go hand in hand. You cannot have faith and not trust. "Trust in the Lord with all your heart and do not lean on your own understanding. In all your ways acknowledge Him, and He will make your paths straight" (Proverbs 3:5-6). That is why we pray, because prayer says, "God, I believe in you and I trust You. I know that You know what I need, and you care very deeply for me."

It is also why we study His Word. We come to know who God is by reading His Word, and He uses His Word to increase our faith. Therein lies the mystery. As we continue to be students of God's Word, He reveals Himself through His Word and teaches us truths that set us free from lies we had believed. Our faith gets stronger, we begin to learn more about God and His love for us, and our love for Him begins to grow. As our love for God grows, our love for others begins to change; and before we know it life takes on new meaning. God changes our attitudes, builds character, and fills our hearts with love, joy, peace, patience, goodness, kindness, gentleness, and temperance. We desire to share what God is doing in our lives; and we begin to stop doing things that hurt people and to find ways to express this newfound love, joy, and peace that permeate our souls. If we continue to set aside a time alone with God each day for Bible study and prayer, God will continue to teach us, to disciple us, and to change us. The enemy does not want us spending time alone with God, because he knows that God will teach us how to overcome his schemes, half-truths, and deceptions. "The thief comes only to steal and kill and destroy; I came that they may have life, and have it abundantly" (John 10:10). Abundant life comes by continuing to trust God, seeking His face through the study of His Word and through prayer. If we fail to do this, our faith will grow weak and we will become the most miserable people on earth. I have seen it too many times and even in my own life. There are no worse people than Christians who have fallen away from the living God. Our time alone with God must be guarded. It is what will make life worth living and even fulfilling. God will fill us with His power as His Holy Spirit continues to work in and through us, bringing glory to God by lives that have been changed.

11

Gifts, Talents and Abilities

G od has given each one of us certain abilities, like being good with your hands, being good with numbers, having a photographic memory, or being of great intelligence. Some have the ability to take things apart and put them back together without help. Some have a natural ability with words and speak eloquently with ease. It is not long before we know what comes easily for us, our special abilities. We also have talents, like being able to play a musical instrument, run fast, catch anything in the wild, or play sports due to great athleticism. Some have the ability to cook really well or have a special way with children or animals, and some can draw or paint astounding beauty on a canvas.

God also gives each one of us a spiritual gift that enables us to edify the people of God. Sometimes we have more than one — like the ability to preach, teach, or speak in tongues, God-given wisdom, healing, service, or faith. Now, all of us have a certain measure of faith; but the gift of faith is when our faith is so great that we never doubt God, His Word, His greatness, or His ability to do the impossible. There are also gifts of encouragement, miracles, and the list goes on. God wants us to use these gifts, talents, and abilities (which are all given to us by Him) to serve people. How will we respond when He asks us what we did with the gifts He gave us to further His kingdom? Will we respond with excuses for what we did not do instead of truths about what we did? Will we be ashamed because we allowed the past to hinder what God wanted to do in and through us? This is known as stubborn pride. When we stand before God, we will not be able to point to others and say, "God, it is because of what he or she did that I was not able to fully use the gifts you gave me to bring glory to you." God has given us the grace, the mercy, and the power to live life to the fullest.

> Do not neglect the spiritual gift within you, which was bestowed on you through prophetic utterance with the laying on of hands by the presbytery. Take pains with these things; be absorbed in them, so that your progress will be evident to all. Pay close attention to yourself and to your teaching; persevere in these things, for as you do this you will ensure salvation both for yourself and for those who hear you (1 Timothy 4:14-16).

God wants to make sure we have everything we need for success. He gives us the power to do the impossible — not for the success of any one individual, but for the success of His church.

> His divine power has given us everything we need for a godly life through our knowledge of him who called us by his own glory and goodness. Through these he has given us his very great and precious promises, so that through them you may participate in the divine nature, having escaped the corruption in the world caused by evil desires (2 Peter 1:3-4 NIV).

84

God has given us everything we need to live godly lives — all we have to do is to choose to live by His power and not our own. It is a daily thing, sometimes minute by minute. If we continue to live for ourselves and be unforgiving, unloving, and focused on self, we will be miserable by our own choice.

A friend of mine told me about a sin in his life that disgusted him; but he was bound by it and did not know how to get it out of his life. Finally, he decided to rid himself of this sin. Every time he sinned, he immediately asked God for forgiveness and for help not to do it again. He told me it seemed like he did this fifty times a day; but, undaunted, he continued to persevere. After the first week, he was only asking God for forgiveness and help about ten times a day; and then by the second week, he was only asking every few days, until this particular sin was eradicated from his life. I believe this is true of all our struggles. If we allow God to deliver us, we have to do our part by asking for forgiveness and for His help, until whatever sin has control over us is no longer part of our lives. It is that simple and yet that hard. It can be done — and God has given us His power to overcome sin. I do not mean that we will never sin; but I do know from personal experience that God can rid our lives of anything we ask of Him. We have to be serious and ready for the fight — our enemy is trying to keep us bound by sin.

> The Lord's bond-servant must not be quarrelsome, but be kind to all, able to teach, patient when wronged, with gentleness correcting those who are in opposition, if perhaps God may grant them repentance leading to the knowledge of the truth, and they may come to their senses and escape from the snare of the devil, having been held captive by him to do his will (2 Timothy 2:24-26)

God again gives us the choice: we can look to Him for His strength and power, or we can be held captive by Satan's will. Anything that keeps us from obedience to God is sin. Satan's will is for us to be bound by hate, living lives filled with bitterness and resentment, with a lust for revenge. You may have heard this before, even thought it or said it yourself: "I will not forgive so-and-so until they come crawling on their hands and knees asking for forgiveness. And then I will spit on them and turn and walk away." This is being held captive by Satan's will — I would rather use the power of the enemy than to depend on God. God sees this as a lack of faith, which stems from unbelief — the worst of sins. Unbelief says, "There is no God, so I can choose to live as I see fit." Unbelief says, "I am my own god." When we choose to disobey God for any reason, we place ourselves among liars, cheaters, murderers, adulterers, rapists, pedophiles, and molesters of the worst kind. When we disobey Him, we are saying, "God, your way is not good enough for me, so I choose to live with hate, bitterness, and resentment. I choose to do what is right in my own eyes. I will decide what is right and wrong for me." Is that what your life is saying? Or are you fighting the good fight of faith and trying to do what God says? Again, it takes dedication, perseverance, trust in God, and the willingness to say, "Not my will, Lord, but Thy will be done." Christianity is not for the faint of heart.

Where Your Treasure Is Your Heart Is Also

In this next passage Paul is talking about the foundation he laid when he shared Christ with people who came to believe and became part of God's church. I want to share what he wants us to understand about an eternal reward for living a godly life.

By the grace God has given me, I laid a foundation
as a wise builder, and someone else is building on
it. But each one should build with care. For no one
can lay any foundation other than the one already
laid, which is Jesus Christ. If anyone builds on this
foundation using gold, silver, costly stones, wood,
hay or straw, their work will be shown for what it
is, because the Day will bring it to light. It will be
revealed with fire, and the fire will test the quality of
each person's work. If what he has built survives, the
builder will receive a reward. If it is burned up, the
builder will suffer loss but yet will be saved — even
though only as one escaping through the flames (1
Corinthians 3:10-15 NIV).

The gold, silver, and costly stones are things that last —
things done for God, things eternal — and of course wood, hay,
and straw are things done in the flesh which will be burned
up. Each of us needs to decide what we are going to do with
the gifts, talents, and abilities God has given us. Are we going
to dig holes and hide our gifts, or will we use them to further
the kingdom of God by the power of His Holy Spirit working
in and through us? God's will is for us to love Him — heart,
mind, soul and strength — and for us to love others with the
same unconditional love that He gives us. We cannot love like
this without the power of His Holy Spirit. God is so excited
about us; He wants us to be all that we can be, and He knows
we need help. Therefore, He wants to be present in us, to fill
our lives with His Holy Spirit. "If the Spirit of Him who raised
Jesus from the dead dwells in you, He who raised Christ Jesus
from the dead will also give life to your mortal bodies through
His Spirit who dwells in you" (Romans 8:11). Because of this, we
have no excuse for disobeying God — He wants us to succeed
and therefore takes up residency within us. Then He tells us

"greater is He who is in you than he who is in the world" (1 John 4:4b). The same power that raised Christ Jesus from the dead dwells in us — wow!

It is impossible to describe or explain God; any attempt is always quite futile. I could say that God is a force, an underlying power, a river of strength for us to call on day and night; and yet, He is so much more. There is nothing that He cannot do to help us in our struggles if we will just call on Him. His pursuit of us is unrelenting as He pours out blessing after blessing, calling us to Himself with a love that can never be matched by any other. He is our creator; He gives us life and breath with every passing moment. "For in Him we live and move and exist . . . 'we also are His children'" (Acts 17:28). We are the children of God; He created us, gives us every breath we take, and allows us every move we make. The moment God decides our time on earth is done, we are ushered into His presence in the heavens to spend eternity with Him. Others will spend eternity without Him. Please do not be one who relies on your own strength. Take a moment and think about all you can do in your own power; and then realize that our God, who has created everything, loves you. The most I am able to create under my own power is one big mess; but I can choose to serve the One who makes the sun to rise and paints the sky blue. I can serve the One who placed the rainbow in the sky after sending the rain. I can choose to follow hard after God and choose to worship Him. And in so doing, God tells me:

> Fight the good fight of faith; take hold of the eternal life to which you were called, and you made the good confession in the presence of many witnesses. I charge you in the presence of God, who gives life to all things, and of Christ Jesus, who testified the good confession before Pontius Pilate, that you keep

the commandment without stain or reproach until the appearing of our Lord Jesus Christ, which He will bring about at the proper time — He who is the blessed and only Sovereign, the King of kings and the Lord of lords, who alone possesses immortality and dwells in unapproachable light, whom no man has seen or can see. To Him be honor and eternal dominion! Amen. (1 Timothy 6:12-16).

Are you fighting the good fight of faith in your own power or in His? Are you relying on the God who is able? Are you choosing to love? Are you using your God-given gifts, talents, and abilities to reach out and love people? It is why God has called us. If Christianity is a crutch, please give me two.

12

Singing Praises to God

When I get a glimpse of how much God loves me, or I begin to realize how much I have been forgiven and all that God has done to bring me into a personal, intimate relationship with Him, I just want to sing. Singing praises to God can do wonderful things for your heart. The Bible says that God inhabits the praises of His people Israel, of which every believer is a part (Psalm 22:3). The truth is that everything we do to please God is an element of our worship. Singing praises to God, reading His Word, actively listening as God's Word is being preached, giving tithes and offerings, lifting prayers, and, yes, even confession of sin.

When I enter the sanctuary, I want to worship God, not worship the things God has done! I am extremely thankful for God's blessings on my life, I am blessed by God daily, and daily I give God thanks. Furthermore, there is no greater gift than to be in a relationship with the One true and living God, which can only be obtained by His grace through faith in His only Son Jesus Christ. For this reason, I enter the congregation with a heart filled with gladness. I come to worship the One True God, and I want to sing to Him — not about what He has done, not about who I am now or who I was before, what I have been through, or even where I am going — I want to praise the name of our God. My heart seems about to explode and I want to say, "God, You are amazing, You are an AWESOME GOD, there is no one like You. I want to praise You, Lord, with my whole heart. I want to worship You in spirit and in truth. Help me to worship You the way You want to be worshipped. I want to love You with all my heart, soul, mind, and strength. Teach me to love You the way You want to be loved."

I want to say this in the songs I sing, because these are my prayers to my Father, to His Son Jesus, and to the Holy Spirit. I want to sing songs that are well thought out and have depth. I do not want to sing one liners over and over again no matter how good it is. I want songs that pour my heart out before an awesome God telling God how awesome He is. I want to worship Him in song with songs that talk about who God is, how great our God is. I do not want to sing songs about what I will do because in truth I know that I fail daily to do God's will. It is the deep well thought songs that sustain me as I go through the week so that I can "let the word of Christ richly dwell within [me], with all wisdom teaching and admonishing one another with psalms and hymns and spiritual songs, singing with thankfulness in [my] heart to God" (Colossians 3:16).

There are so many great songs that can bring me right to the throne of God — songs that express exactly what my heart wants to say, like singing about God's faithfulness or songs that talk about how great our God is. Songs that talk about adoring the Creator, songs that are sung directly to God make my heart sore. I really wonder about the time we come to worship and we sing songs about God like He is not present with us. We sing songs to God in third person like we are telling the person next to us when they are singing the same thing. It just does not make any sense to me. I want to come into God's presence singing songs that are speaking directly to the heart of God. The mystery is that while we are singing to Him, our hearts are lifted out of whatever suffering and pain we are enduring, and joy fills us. Our focus changes from who we are to who God is. We no longer dwell on bad situations or difficult circumstances because we are lost in worship of our King. Worship involves adoration, love devotion and reverence of God. Worship gives God the highest place in our lives. Many times when I choose to worship God through a heart filled with pain it does not sound like worship — but it is! In these times we choose to worship God even when we do not feel like it, even in the midst of pain and suffering, which I believe is the highest form of praise and worship. Has your worship of God ever been interrupted by your tears? You cannot sing the words anymore because you are so overwhelmed, but the melody continues in your heart and the words continue in your mind. That is worship! I have experienced this during congregational singing and even praising God through songs on my own, and there are no greater times of worship that I can remember. Songs sung directly to the Lord of heaven and earth fill my heart with joy and my mouth with praise. It is electrifying. God's presence becomes so strong that you just do not want to quit. This is what church is all about; this is why we come — so that we can enter His presence with singing, offering songs directly to God, with hearts filled with worship of God, in awe of God. I believe this prepares us for the message that is going to be shared from the Word of God. Because we have been in God's presence, we are aware of His presence all around us. His holiness pierces our hearts, and we have to stop for a moment as we confess the sins we are being convicted of before we can rejoin the congregation in singing. As we continue to sing, the people of God begin to be convicted of un-confessed sin, because in His presence sin is revealed. We confess, and God strips us of guilt and shame. Then, with holy hearts filled with His Spirit, we begin to sing out. We have been renewed and refreshed, and we just cannot help it. As the Holy Spirit of God moves through the congregation, our lives are filled with wonder and awe of Him; and with one heart and one mind we truly worship. Worship God alone.

13

Suffering

I want to share about worship from a life touched by hurt and pain and suffering. I know a woman who remarried later in life. They decided to have a child, even though she had already raised two children who were now grown and out of the house. All in one year she had three children. The first died shortly after birth, the second miscarried after a few short months, and the third died three and a half days after birth — and on her birthday — even though she lay in a hospital bed for several days after her water had broken in order to give this baby a better chance of living. To make things even worse, her young niece and her husband (who both spent a lot of time stoned) were given a strong baby boy; a short time later, a beautiful little girl; and then another boy.

Now, why did God allow this to happen? I assure you, any answers you may have will not assuage the pain in this woman's life. She was deeply hurt, asking "Why?" and God was no longer real to her. In fact, she would tell you there is no god. God would not give a drug-addicted couple three beautiful children to live lives of abuse and take away three beautiful children from an experienced mother who has a great heart full of love. Why did all this happen? There are no answers. I could sit here and write trite responses like "Everything happens for a reason." I hear this so often, and it hurts to hear something so empty and heartless. Or how about "They are not suffering anymore," "God is in control." We already know these things — why is it so difficult for people to sit silently by and grieve with us. Trite, benign sayings will not make someone who is suffering feel any better. Time does not heal all wounds we just learn to cope.

My least favorite saying is "God will not give us more than we can handle." This is not Biblical. Please show me where the Bible says this. If God did not give us more than we could handle, then why would we need Him? The truth is that God allows us to take on more than we can handle and then stands by to see if we will call on Him for help. There are other times that life deals out more pain, abuse, or torment than any one person can handle, and the only way through the pain is by trusting God.

We cannot overcome difficult and trying times with joy, hope, and peace without a personal, intimate relationship with the living God. The woman I mentioned earlier has since returned to a loving relationship with God the Father in spite of all that she has had to endure. Her life is still far from perfect — deeply painful trials are still present in her life, but she knows only God can do the impossible. She is trusting God to continue working in her life and in her family. She has become a prayer warrior and continues to grow in wisdom and knowledge of the mysterious ways of God. She is a person of peace, looking for God to restore her family. She has chosen love, clings to hope, and does what she feels God is leading her to do. She does not push and is not demanding but lives her life by the grace of God. How many others have stories of a similar nature — of broken hearts due to sexual, physical, mental, or emotional abuse, a wayward child, or the loss of a loved one? How many people are suffering because of pain caused by another? I daresay most of us can tell stories about people who have broken our hearts, hurt us deeply, and left us looking for a way to pick up the pieces. Our hearts get broken most deeply by those we love the most.

Regardless of the reason, broken hearts seem to lead us into brokenness, depression, and despair. Instead of looking to God for a way through the pain, we look for a way out of it and usually get our hearts broken again and again. We look to other people, or we get involved in work, drugs, video games, television, shopping, and a host of other things that only seem to push the pain aside. Furthermore, there is not even the tiniest measure of healing found in any of those things. Most of the time, we dwell on the pain and those who caused it — falling into depression filled with torment due to the hurt, and finding our lives filled with hate, bitterness, and resentment. Believe it or not, those who are guilty of breaking hearts and homes follow the same path. Sadly, it is often only while looking back over the devastation caused by broken promises, selfishness, bitterness, ignoring God and worshiping self that we realize the depth of our depravity. Like me, many have come from broken homes, abuses of every type, and trying to live on our own power, only to repeat this evil process again and again. This is what God is speaking of when He teaches us about the sins of the fathers.

Sins of the Father

The commandments of God, which are given to teach us how to love God and love others, direct us to have no other gods before Him. We should not make any graven image to bow down to in worship, and we should not have any idols. God tells us it is because He is a jealous God and wants His creation to worship Him, not creation or any man-made thing. God says when we give our worship to any other, then He will visit the iniquity of the fathers on our children to the third and fourth generations. This is found in Exodus chapter 20 and again in Deuteronomy chapter 5. The sins of our fathers are real. Have you ever noticed that we pass on certain good and bad characteristics to our children? When the bad ones are passed on, they seem to have a greater detrimental effect, holding our children in an even greater struggle. Sometimes when a child grows up with an alcoholic parent they become an even worse alcoholic. On the other hand, they may never take a drink because of their childhood; but some other bad behavior may become their undoing. Not only do we pass our sinful struggles on to our children, but we also pass our sickness and diseases on to them.

> But it shall come about, if you do not obey the Lord your God, to observe to do all His commandments and His statutes with which I charge you today, that all these curses will come upon you and overtake you: Cursed shall you be in the city, and cursed shall you be in the country. Cursed shall be your basket and your kneading bowl. Cursed shall be the offspring of your body and the produce of your ground, the increase of your herd and the young of your flock. Cursed shall you be when you come in, and cursed shall you be when you go out. The Lord will send upon you curses, confusion, and rebuke, in all you undertake to do, until you are destroyed and until you perish quickly, on account of the evil of your deeds, because you have forsaken Me. The Lord will make the pestilence cling to you until He has consumed you

from the land where you are entering to possess it. The Lord will smite you with consumption and with fever and with inflammation and with fiery heat and with the sword and with the blight and with mildew, and they will pursue you until you perish. The heaven which is over your head shall be bronze, and the earth which is under you, iron. The Lord will make the rain of your land powder and dust; from heaven it shall come down on you until you are destroyed. The Lord shall cause you to be defeated before your enemies; you will go out one way against them, but you will flee seven ways before them, and you will be an example of terror to all the kingdoms of the earth. Your carcasses will be food to all birds of the sky and to the beasts of the earth, and there will be no one to frighten them away (Deuteronomy 28:15-26).

Can you see any of these curses in your life today? Do not think that just because this is in the Old Testament that it does not apply to us today. A good friend of mine reminded me that pain in childbearing and men working by the sweat of their brow are still a reality and they are the first two curses upon man for sin (Genesis 3:16-19). The chapter quoted above goes on for sixty-eight verses. God is serious about obedience to Him. We can choose His way or our own — and I can tell you that our own way is much harder than choosing to serve Almighty God, who loves us more than we can ever imagine. But if we choose to serve ourselves through these false gods that demand we choose all that is ugly, repulsive toward God, demeaning, obnoxious, hostile, and abusive, then we are no better than those who have hurt us to begin with. We have now become the abusers — insisting those who have hurt us do what we say, when we say, and how we say, without any promise of forgiveness. We try to place them into a prison of our own making so that they will suffer the way we have suffered. The truth is, we do not have that power. We have suffered because we have chosen to ignore the Living God, who tells us to forgive and be set free. It is not possible to pour upon them the pain, anguish, misery, torment, agony, and affliction that we have experienced. God has not given us that power.

Finding the Way Out

There is a way out, but it is not an easy one. It is a hard and elusive thing called forgiveness — and it can only be obtained through the power of God. Forgiveness is indeed divine, and it will set you free. God even asks us to go further in our forgiveness by giving blessings. I have already quoted this Scripture once, but it is worth hearing again. Maybe if we wrote this on our bathroom mirrors where we would see it every day while getting ready for the day, it would begin to sink in.

> Love must be sincere. Hate what is evil; cling to what is good. Be devoted to one another in love. Honor one another above yourselves. Never be lacking in zeal, but keep your spiritual fervor, serving the Lord. Be joyful in hope, patient in affliction, faithful in prayer. Share with the Lord's people who are in need. Practice hospitality. Bless those who persecute you; bless and do not curse. Rejoice with those who rejoice; mourn with those who mourn. Live in harmony with one another. Do not be proud, but be willing to associate with people of low position. Do not be conceited. Do not repay anyone evil for evil. Be careful to do what is right in the eyes of everyone. If it is possible, as far as it depends on you, live at peace with everyone. Do not take revenge, my dear friends, but leave room for God's wrath, for it is written: "It is mine to

avenge; I will repay," says the Lord. On the contrary; "If your enemy is hungry, feed him; if he is thirsty, give him something to drink. In doing this, you will heap burning coals on his head. Do not be overcome by evil, but overcome evil with good (Romans 12:9-21 NIV).

We will never win the battle until we realize that it is our enemy, the devil, who uses people to hurt us; and then he uses our emotions and feelings to destroy us.

Finally, be strong in the Lord and in the strength of His might. Put on the full armor of God, so that you will be able to stand firm against the schemes of the devil. For our struggle is not against flesh and blood, but against the rulers, against the powers, against the world forces of this darkness, against the spiritual forces of wickedness in the heavenly places. Therefore, take up the full armor of God, so that you will be able to resist in the evil day, and having done everything, to stand firm (Ephesians 6:10-13).

God wants to be a part of our daily lives. He wants us to live moment by moment trusting Him. If we try to live in our own strength, we will fail. If we spend all of life focusing on everything bad that has happened to us, we will live lives filled with torment. That is right, torment — bitterness, resentment, hate, anger and a host of other things. Which do you prefer? You get to choose. You can continue down the road to destruction, focusing on your past and dwelling on the suffering life brings; or you can choose God's way. If you choose God, then you are choosing to focus on Him, to live through the mighty power of His Holy Spirit working in and through you. You are choosing to read His Word daily so that you can be set free from your past. You are choosing to allow God to speak to you through His Word, encouraging you, comforting you, and teaching you how He wants you to live.

Many times we are quick to believe that it is the devil's handiwork that keeps us down; but in reality we stay down because we choose it. We say we cannot overcome because of all we have done wrong or because of all the wrong that has been done to us. It is pride that keeps us from change, that tells us to stay the way we are and blame others. Remember, unforgiveness is a sin.

> Therefore humble yourselves under the mighty hand of God, that He may exalt you at the proper time, casting all your anxiety on Him, because He cares for you. Be of sober spirit, be on the alert. Your adversary, the devil, prowls around like a roaring lion, seeking someone to devour. But resist him, firm in your faith, knowing that the same experiences of suffering are being accomplished by your brethren who are in the world. After you have suffered for a little while, the God of all grace, who called you to His eternal glory in Christ, will Himself perfect, confirm, strengthen and establish you. To Him be dominion forever and ever. Amen (1 Peter 5:6-11).

Your enemy wants to destroy you — not just take a bite out of you, but destroy you. Jesus says, "The thief comes only to steal and kill and destroy; I came that they may have life, and have it abundantly" (John 10:10). You get to choose who you will live for — Jesus or the enemy. We get to choose blessings or curses. Everyone experiences suffering, because it is a part of life. Some of us have experienced great suffering and have learned to overcome the pain and torment by trusting God, who is present with us. He can help if we will only invite Him to be part of our suffering. When we invite God (through prayer) to give us the strength to overcome, He will; but He will also require us to continue seeking Him, moment by moment and day by day, until that day we stand before Him.

> I call heaven and earth to witness against you today, that I have set before you life and death, the blessing and the curse. So choose life in order that you may live, you and your descendants, by loving the Lord you God, by obeying His voice, and by holding fast to Him; for this is your life and the length of your days (Deuteronomy 30:19-20a).

Choose This Day Whom You Will Serve

Years ago, someone used two huge sweet gum trees as part of a fence with a gate that is long since gone. Both trees have scars where five strands of barbed wire went completely around them. The barbed wire can no longer be seen, except for a strand or two that was not cut off and sticks out a few inches. The rest of the barbed wire is deep within each tree. Each tree grew over and enveloped the barbed wire, covering it with bark and the core of the tree. One has two hinges that are still visible, though old and rusted, and the tree is about fifty feet tall and still growing strong. The other one is about 35 feet tall and dead. It makes me think about how our hurts and pains scar our lives. What we do with those scars will be the difference in living or dying. If we choose life, we grow stronger and stand taller. We choose the hard road, learning to forgive and focusing on things that breathe life into us. We do these things because we know it is what God wants us to do. God blesses obedience, and therefore we know that God will honor our choices and help us by His Spirit living within us. We become compassionate, understanding, full of wisdom and knowledge, because we know pain, how to overcome it, and how not be overcome by it. "'Not by power, nor by might, but by My Spirit,' says the Lord" (Zechariah 4:6b). We focus on the One who will help us endure, persevere, and finally overcome. We still have scars, but you would never know it. God has grown us into people of character who would rather choose meekness (great power under control) and humility (a godly attribute few have mastered). Our hearts are filled with love. This type of response is what God desires and is the truest form of worship.

The sad thing is that some of us will choose to focus on those scars and those who caused them. These are the walking dead — hateful, demanding, critical, overbearing, full of pride and arrogance. We are under the assumption that holding a grudge gives us some sort of power over the one who hurt us, which helps us cope. But the truth is that we are miserable; and, since misery loves company, we often make those around us miserable. Living this way invites sickness and disease which affect our minds, bodies, and spirits. Even more disturbing is the fact that we pass this type of behavior on to our children. This is why God commands us to forgive. Here is the mystery once again: forgiveness sets *us* free — not those who hurt us but we who have been hurt. Forgiveness is for the forgiver, and there is no forgiveness without forgiveness. We need to choose God's way and look to Him for help.

> For God, who said, 'Light shall shine out of darkness,'
> is the One who has shone in our hearts to give the
> Light of the knowledge of the glory of God in the
> face of Christ. But we have this treasure in earthen

vessels, so that the surpassing greatness of the power will be of God and not from ourselves; we are afflicted in every way, but not crushed; perplexed, but not despairing; persecuted, but not forsaken; struck down, but not destroyed; always carrying about in the body the dying of Jesus, so that the life of Jesus also may be manifested in our body. For we who live are constantly being delivered over to death for Jesus' sake, so that the life of Jesus also may be manifested in our mortal flesh. So death works in us, but life in you (2 Corinthians 4:6-12)

I know by these verses that there is a purpose in our suffering. It gives me great comfort to know that my suffering may be able to touch a life in a way that it will be changed forever. By reading God's Word, our hearts can find comfort. God can also increase our faith through His Word. "Therefore, those also who suffer according to the will of God shall entrust their souls to a faithful Creator in doing what is right" (1 Peter 4:19). Wow! "Those who suffer according to the will of God." Can you imagine that there is suffering according to the will of God? He wants to change our focus, helping us concentrate on Him and on His desire for us instead of on self. We cannot love God with all our minds without getting to know Him through His Word. We cannot love Him with all our minds if we choose to dwell on the past. God wants His truth to permeate our lives.

"So Jesus was saying to those Jews who had believed Him, 'If you continue in My word, then you are truly disciples of Mine; and you will know the truth, and the truth will make you free" (John 8:31b-32). Do you want to be free from your past? Then look to God.

> Hear my cry, O God; give heed to my prayer. From the end of the earth I call to You when my heart is faint; lead me to the rock that is higher than I. For You have been a refuge for me, a tower of strength against the enemy. Let me dwell in Your tent forever; let me take refuge in the shelter of Your wings (Psalm 61:1-4).

God wants to tell each of us many more wonderful things; but maybe it is time for you to dust off your Bible and get reacquainted with the Most High God. He is waiting and looking forward to spending time alone with you.

> Rejoice in the Lord always; again I will say, rejoice! Let your gentle spirit be known to all men. The Lord is near. Be anxious for nothing, but in everything by prayer and supplication with thanksgiving let your requests be made known to God. And the peace of God, which surpasses all comprehension, will guard your hearts and your minds in Christ Jesus. Finally, brethren, whatever is true, whatever is honorable, whatever is right, whatever is pure, whatever is lovely, whatever is of good repute, if there is any excellence and if anything worthy of praise, dwell on these things. The things you have learned and received and heard and seen in me, practice these things, and the God of peace will be with you (Philippians 4:4-9).

14

The Church

I wonder how God feels when we decide we are not going to go to church because someone hurt our feelings. We make excuses so that we do not have to go through what it takes to build relationships — forgiving, understanding, and working toward reconciliation. It is much easier to blame someone else for our shortcomings than to do what we know God wants us to do. Reconciliation is not always possible, since we can only be responsible for our own actions; but building relationships, sharing together, praying for each other, learning to love the unlovable . . . that is worship. The truth is that sometimes we are the unlovable ones. We need to keep something in mind here. When we are having trouble in relationships we need to remember that "[our] adversary, the devil, prowls around like a roaring lion, seeking someone to devour" (1 Peter 5:8b). If the devil can destroy relationships, he can tear down the church from the inside — but only if we let him. This is why it is so important to be reconciled to each other. We are not always going to agree, get along, or have the same beliefs; but we can agree to disagree. We can search the Scriptures to see what the Bible says about what we believe. We can build and strengthen relationships through in-depth Bible study, studying the Word of God together.

This is giving God the ultimate authority by seeking the truth in His Word. God is glorified when we choose to work through our problems instead of running from them because someone hurt our feelings. "My brethren, if any among you strays from the truth and one turns him back, let him know that he who turns a sinner from the error of his way will save a soul from death and will cover a multitude of sins" (James 5:19-20). A multitude of sins can be covered by discovering truth together. God's Word is truth! The Bible says "we wrestle not against flesh and blood, but against principalities, against powers, against the rulers of the darkness of this world, against spiritual wickedness in high places" (Ephesians 6:12 KJV). God is telling us here that we are battling the devil, his dark powers, and those who follow him. There are those Satan uses to do his will; and, sadly enough, some of these people are in the church, with no desire to be obedient to God or filled with His Holy Spirit. What is even worse is that, when we choose to live outside of God's will, we are being used by Satan! "Submit therefore to God. Resist the devil and he will flee from you. Draw near to God and he will draw near to you. Cleanse your hands, you sinners; and purify your hearts, you double-minded. Be miserable and mourn and weep; let your laughter be turned into mourning and your joy to gloom. Humble yourselves in the presence of the Lord, and He will exalt you" (James 4:7-10). God gives us the remedy to overcome, which is to draw near to Him. If we resist the devil, he will flee — God will make sure of it. He wants us to be part of a church: serving together, worshipping together, praying together, and growing in our faith together. In fact, our faith is increased every time God's Word is preached over us. "Faith comes by hearing, and hearing by the word of God" (Romans 10:17 KJV).

The "One Another's"

Another reason God wants us to be together is that we are strengthened by relationships — people can pray for us and we for them. We can have fellowship together: share our problems, our hopes, our dreams. We can share our doubts, our fears, and our struggles. We can share our praises and encourage each other. There is strength in numbers, and we are all part of God's holy army. We can praise God corporately, which is one of the greatest encouragements we will ever experience this side of heaven. God tells us, "Let us hold fast the confession of our hope without wavering, for He who promised is faithful; and let us consider how to stimulate one another to love and good deeds, not forsaking our own assembling together, as is the habit of some, but encouraging one another; and all the more as you see the day drawing near" (Hebrews 10:23-25). This verse is describing church, the gathering together of God's saints. If you are a follower of Jesus Christ, then you are a saint of God whether you feel like it or not, because God says so. So let us start acting like saints and work at loving people with the same unconditional love that God continues to pour out on us. "Brethren, even if anyone is caught in any trespass, you who are spiritual, restore such a one in a spirit of gentleness; each one looking to yourself, so that you too will not be tempted" (Galatians 6:1). Is there anyone in the church willing to be spiritual? If you are a student of the Word of God, then you are spiritual. If you believe in God, pray, and read His Word, you are spiritual. If you pray and ask God to help you love Him and worship Him in spirit and in truth, you are spiritual. What are you waiting for? Let's work at being spiritual.

Read Philippians chapter 2 and see the kind of people that God is calling us to be. The Bible says we should not think too highly of ourselves and that we should think more highly of others. I think we have this backward in most of our relationships. We are more concerned about what we can get from a relationship then what we can give. We are more interested in being right than living in harmony. We are more concerned about how we are treated than how we treat others. Listen to what God desires: "The Lord's bond-servant must not be quarrelsome, but be kind to all, able to teach, patient when wronged, with gentleness correcting those who are in opposition, if perhaps God may grant them repentance leading to the knowledge of the truth, and they may come to their senses and escape from the snare of the devil, having been held captive by him to do his will" (2 Timothy 2:24-26). God wants to use us to set the captives free. He wants us to be gentle and kind, using His Word to teach truth to those who are held captive by lies and half-truths. That is why the church is so important, because we learn how to be the type of servant that God wants us to be. We become part of the family of God, and He uses us to love people.

Our church family is there to help us, encourage us, pray for us; and as our lives become intertwined, we begin to be the ones who help, pray for, and encourage others. We cannot do the "one another's" mentioned throughout the New Testament without being part of a church. Each one of us needs to make a diligent search for a church where the Word of God is preached and time is given for prayer, the reading of the Scriptures, and singing praise to God. If we ask, God will help us to find the church where He wants us. I cannot tell you the number of times someone tells me that they can worship anywhere they want, that they do not need to be in a church. They tell me they can worship under a tree somewhere. The truth is, they are right — but they won't. Find a church and allow God to use you to bless others and others to bless you.

15

Encouragement

Have you ever noticed what happens whenever you give someone an encouraging word? It can make their day. Once I told someone that what they did glorified God. Later, I heard this person tell others how encouraged they were by what I said, which immediately encouraged me. Therein lies the mystery. When you give encouragement, not only does it make that person feel good, but it also makes you, the giver, feel good. Many times our encouragement is like a word from the Lord. The truth is that God puts it in our hearts to encourage others. "Let your speech always be with grace, as though seasoned with salt, so that you will know how you should respond to each person" (Colossians 4:6). "Let your light shine before men in such a way that they may see your good works, and glorify your Father who is in heaven" (Matthew 5:16). Tell someone today that the good work they are doing gives glory to God, and watch what happens. You will make their day. There is enough negativity around us, bringing us down time and time again. We need people who watch and listen for opportunities to be encouraging.

I often hear people saying bad things about others. Rarely do I hear anyone defending the person but, instead, joining in the conversation — tearing people down instead of building them up. This type of conversation causes strife and hatefulness, bringing stress into the lives of those who participate. Sometimes we say hurtful things and then say that we are only kidding. These things we say when "only kidding" still hurt, and there is usually a lot of truth in what we say. Many times what we say in jest we say from a heart that has been hurt, and this is our way of getting even. When we make derogatory statements about someone, whether kidding or not, feelings get hurt. The person may even say, "I know they are just kidding," but do not fool yourself — it hurts. Encouragement, on the other hand, builds up and makes everyone involved feel good and right. It is much harder to look and listen for the good in a person than it is to say negative and degrading things. The negative comes naturally, but it takes good strong moral character to look beyond the shortcomings of people to find the good and the positive. What would our homes, schools, workplaces, and other places we frequent look and feel like if we obeyed God's instruction. "Let your speech always be with grace as though seasoned with salt" (Colossians 4:5a). Have you given much thought to what salt does? Salt makes food taste better; it also preserves food. Do we give enough thought to what we are going to say in order to bless the ones who are listening? Is our speech seasoned with salt and touched by grace?

As believers, we are called to be examples of Christ, who tells us, "So, as those who have been chosen of God, holy and beloved, put on a heart of compassion, kindness, humility, gentleness and patience; bearing with one another, and forgiving each other, whoever has a complaint against anyone; just as the Lord forgave you, so also should you" (Colossians

3:12-13). These are difficult rules to live by — it can only be done through the power of the Holy Spirit of God. If we want to live by these rules, we will need God's power working in and through us. Ask God to show you the positive attributes in a person's life so you can encourage them, and He will. In the book of Ephesians, Paul wrote, "Therefore I, the prisoner of the Lord, implore you to walk in a manner worthy of the calling with which you have been called, with all humility and gentleness, with patience, showing tolerance for one another in love, being diligent to preserve the unity of the Spirit in the bond of peace. There is one body and one Spirit, just as also you were called in one hope of your calling; one Lord, one faith, one baptism, one God and Father of all who is over all and through all and in all" (Ephesians 4:1-6). Does it not encourage us to know that the God who is Father of all, over all, and through all, is also in all of us? Give an encouraging word to someone today — really look for something specific about them that will be more meaningful.

16

Giving

Here is something that should truly make you stop and think. First I need to tell you what most Christians already know — simply that you cannot out-give God. In fact, the Bible says, "It is more blessed to give than to receive" (Acts 20:35b). But God does not stop here. Jesus says, "Give, and it will be given to you. They will pour into your lap a good measure — pressed down, shaken together, and running over. For by your standard of measure it will be measured to you in return" (Luke 6:38). Did you notice that? By your standard of measure it will be given back. That means if you give freely and in abundance, it will be given to you freely and in abundance. Guess who has more to give? This means we do not have to be the glass-half-full or glass-half-empty kind of people. We can be filled up, pressed down, shaken together, overflowing people. Our cups can always be overflowing when we choose to be giving people. Plus, money is not the only thing we can give. We can give of our time, lend things, or give hand-me-down clothes, toys, or other things. Instead of trying to sell the things we have replaced, we should look for someone in need and give. God wants to bless us, but He wants us to be a blessing to others.

And make sure that once you give a gift, you must realize it is no longer yours, and it should not matter how it is used. If I choose to give or not to give because I am afraid of what they might spend it on, then I have become a judge. We give in obedience to God; how that gift is used is not our concern or responsibility. We give because we want to bless God and His people — and all of creation are God's people. A person might not believe in God or claim they know God, but of this one thing you can be sure: God claims them as His, so give. If that person wants to spend what you gave them on drugs or alcohol or whatever foolishness they choose, what is that to you? God put it in your heart to give, so give. God wants to bless us. The more we give, the more God will give. And when God gives, it is not just monetary; He gives spiritual gifts as well. He blesses our lives with peace and joy. God can make our lives exciting as we give — not only monetarily, but as we share Christ with people as well. We teach people what God has done in our lives and how He continues to sustain us with His love, mercy, and grace. These same gifts are for everyone who wants to believe and trust in Him. God wants to bless our lives, the lives of our children, and the lives of our children's children if we will just give Him our all. The Bible says, "Know therefore that the Lord your God, He is God, the faithful God, who keeps His covenant and His lovingkindness to a thousandth generation with those who love Him and keep His commandments" (Deuteronomy 7:9). How great is it to know that our obedience can make a difference, not only in our children's lives, but to a thousand generations?

God wants to bless us above and beyond anything we can even imagine — not just with money but with life, abundant life. We can break the cycle of sin by choosing to be obedient, and not just in giving but by choosing a life dedicated to loving people. Giving love — this is God's desire for each one of us, because it is what God is dedicated to. God loves people and "desires all men to be saved and to come to the knowledge of the truth" (1 Timothy 2:4). His desire is that all should know Christ. "The Lord is not slow about His promise, as some count slowness, but is patient toward you, not wishing for any to perish but for all to come to repentance" (2 Peter 3:9). When we understand how great God is and how God loves to give, we have to realize that God gave the greatest gift in His Son Jesus Christ. Jesus died for the sins of the world. He gave His all by dying on the cross so that we could live — the greatest personal sacrifice ever given. We can give of our time, our money, our wisdom and knowledge. We can choose to work for free for someone in need. We can spend time with people who are lonely; we can help someone who needs it. God puts people in our lives so that we can share the blessings that He has given us.

For many years I worked as a mechanic, and there were certain church members I chose to give my labor to without charge. I wanted to give of my time in order to be a blessing to them and give a blessing to God. However, some other people in the church got mad at me because of how much I normally charged them for my services. the truth is we should want to pay our Christian brother and sisters for their services because they are fair and honest. We should never run people down regardless of what we believe they should be doing. It is best for us to work in a way that please God. We should do our work in a way that brings glory to God. Another hindrance was that someone would have a car question for me on any given Sunday morning and I would stand in the foyer trying to help them. It was not fair to me since they had all week to call me and I would gladly help them fix their car without charge by giving them the information they needed. I love to teach people how to fix their car but this robbed me of worship. I came to church to sing praises and to hear the Word of God preached and to encourage people but instead I was held at bay, just outside the doors of the sanctuary, talking about cars. In saying this I am asking people not to ask fix-it questions at church. Most Christian workers are more than happy to teach someone how to do something for themselves — just bring these questions during the work week.

Furthermore, we should pay our Christian workers top dollar in order to keep them in business. We should pay them the same price we would pay any other professional. It is what God would have us to do. If I choose to give someone a break on a price, it is because I feel led by God to do so. The Bible says "the worker is worthy of his support" (Matthew 10:10). This is true of our pastors, who are diligent to prepare for the message they will deliver, the singing they will lead, or the children they will teach — they are worthy of their wages. We, the congregation, are to bless without reservation, not holding back. There are more ways than you can count to give — we just need to open our eyes, look around, and obey God as He pricks our hearts and says "Give."

17

The Tithe

Another gift we give, known in Christian circles as the tithe, is something we do to show our trust in God with our money. For many people, money is our most prized possession — at least you would think it is, judging by how tightfisted we are with it (unless, of course, we are spending it on ourselves). God asks us to give a portion of every bit of money that we are given — a paycheck, a gift — any money that is ours. Now here is where the mystery comes in. If we choose not to give God charge over our money, this is what happens: we never have enough to make ends meet. We work hard, we work overtime, we work multiple jobs, and still we live from paycheck to paycheck. Why? The book of Haggai says, "'You have sown much, but harvest little; you eat, but there is not enough to be satisfied; you drink, but there is not enough to become drunk; you put on clothing, but no one is warm enough; and he who earns, earns wages to put into a purse with holes . . . You look for much, but behold, it comes to little; when you bring it home, I blow it away. Why?' declares the Lord of hosts, 'Because of My house which lies desolate, while each of you runs to his own house'" (Haggai 1:6, 9). We must realize that God provides money for us to live on, and it is His desire that we give a portion of it back to Him, to the church where we are being fed. We are fed bread from heaven — the Bread of Life, Jesus. The church feeds us spiritually, and our spiritual house is built up by the preaching of God's Word. We are encouraged by belonging to something that is bigger than ourselves. We give in order to build up the kingdom of God and help provide for others. And we give so that our pastors can eat and live as well.

When we give God a portion of our money, even when we think we do not have enough, somehow we are able to make it though the month with all our bills paid and, many times, with some left over. This is another mystery of God — what little we have is enough when we are living in obedience to Him. It is not for us to compare what we do or do not have, but to trust God. Have you ever noticed how much misery money can bring when we do not manage it well? Now, I want to add an addendum here. When we come to believe in God, put our trust in Him, and live in obedience to Him, we will still struggle through life. Things will still go wrong — we will still be tried, we will still face problems. The only difference is that God is with us, helping us stand up and persevere through trials, test and tribulations. The mystery continues here, only it gets better because the living God helps us to persevere; and we become people of character whose lives reflect God's glory.

People notice those who have been through trials and have walked through the fire with God. Now God uses these people to help others who face some of the same struggles. Read what God says through Paul:

> Nevertheless, the firm foundation of God stands, having this seal, "The Lord knows those who are His," and, "Everyone who names the name of the

Lord is to abstain from wickedness." Now in a large house there are not only gold and silver vessels, but also vessels of wood and of earthenware, and some to honor and some to dishonor. Therefore, if anyone cleanses himself from these things, he will be a vessel for honor, sanctified, useful to the Master, prepared for every good work (2 Timothy 2:19-21).

God knows those who are His; and He continues to work in our lives, making us vessels of honor — vessels that God is proud to use to do His work here on earth. Do you want to be used by God? If you are a believer, you are already being used; you are also being tested, tried, and purified into precious children of God. You are a child of the King — the King of kings and the Lord of Lords. You are royalty. We should want to bless God by giving ourselves away to help others. The biggest reason the tithe is so important is because we are being obedient to God. God blesses obedience. Giving a tithe says we trust God. It also furthers ministry — the tithe pays our pastors, music ministers, youth and children's leaders. It buys books for us to study in order to learn more about God and His Word. Some of the tithe is used for missions here and abroad. This is just a small picture of how much the tithe can do. If your church uses the tithe wisely, it is being used to support people in ministry and provide necessary resources to do ministry. We need to be obedient and give.

18

Pride

H ere is a fact that I hope will help us to walk in obedience to God: our enemy the devil was kicked out of heaven because of pride. Pride is a prison that we should want to avoid. It says, "I am better than you. I don't need anyone — I can do it myself." An arrogant pride looks down on others, belittles, and condescends. It says, "I am the greatest. The world owes me." We may turn to pride in order to be set free from the pain of our past. Pride chooses to hate those who have wronged us and look for ways to get back, to retaliate, to get revenge. We begin to believe that these things give us power over the past. Yet all this is the opposite of how God wants us to respond. He tells us to let go of the past and look forward to the high calling that He has on each of our lives. He tells us to forgive and be set free. Often we choose to follow the path of self-destruction that comes from being imprisoned by our past. We fall deeper and deeper into sickness, depression, and disease because we choose to dwell on the past instead of changing our focus to the One who can heal us. What would happen if we spent most of our driving time looking in a tiny rear-view mirror and very little time looking out of the huge front windshield? It would not be long before our vehicles would crash. If we continue to drive this way, we would be in one wreck after another until our cars were totally destroyed. The same is true if we choose to allow the past to dictate who we are — we will fall and fail time and time again. Anxiety and depression will rule our lives. We will become trapped in prisons of our own making because we have chosen to hate instead of asking God to help us love.

Pride says, "Look at me, look at me. Look at how great I am!" Unfortunately, you see this often on the ball field when a player thumps his chest and stomps his feet, saying to those watching, "I am the greatest." What they fail to notice is how many others helped them reach this level of achievement — their parents, coaches, fellow team members, and, of course, God, who blessed them with certain gifts, talents, and abilities. I love football and I enjoy those who can make a great play and then just go back to the huddle — those who have great athleticism and do not feel the need to do the "Look at me, look at me!" thing are the ones who impress me. The old adage seems to have been lost: It is amazing how much could be accomplished if people did not care who got the credit. No, now people are quick to point out who made the goal, who figured out the problem, or who came up with the bright idea. In truth, it is God who gave us minds to think, talents for greatness, abilities to astound, and spiritual gifts to touch the lives of those around us. The true purpose of all that God has given us is for glorifying God and encouraging each other.

The Body of Christ

That is what the church is supposed to look like — a team working together to make sure no one is left behind. Everybody's needs are being met; those who have an abundance share with those who have nothing. Those who have nothing meet needs with their God-given gifts, talents, and abilities as well. That is why it is called the body of Christ. Everybody has a job to do in order for the body to work together for the good of the whole. Everyone uses their God-given qualities for edification. People work together with a great love for God and for people. Have you ever noticed that the Ten Commandments are all about love? The first four commandments show us how we are to love God and the next six how we are to love one another. If we love those around us, we will not steal from them, covet what they have, tell lies, or murder. No — we will give, we will choose to love, we will look for ways to glorify God; and in the process, the people around us get their needs met. When everyone works together, looking for ways to use their gifts, talents, and abilities for the benefit of others, God is being glorified! The angels of heaven are jumping up and down, saying, "Look at that one go!" I can just imagine them high-fiving in amazement, watching someone who is not looking for earthly praise but is doing everything for the audience of One. He is watching! Who will you give your glory to — God or self? That is right — living the Christian life is not for the faint of heart.

"Do nothing from selfishness or empty conceit, but with humility of mind regard one another as more important than yourselves (Philippians 2:3)." Being proud or arrogant is easy and even natural; humility, on the other hand, takes great character. "For through the grace given to me I say to everyone among you not to think more highly of himself than he ought to think; but to think so as to have sound judgment, as God has allotted to each a measure of faith" (Romans 12:3). Many of us think way too highly of ourselves, and because of this pride our relationships are damaged. "It is not good to eat too much honey, nor is it honorable to search out matters that are too deep" (Proverbs 25:27 NIV). "Let us not lose heart in doing good, for in due time we will reap if we do not grow weary. So then, while we have opportunity, let us do good to all people, and especially to those who are of the household of faith" (Galatians 6:9-10). These verses speak of a humble heart that wants to live for God and lay up treasures in heaven. This type of person does not seek the praises of men but the praises of God.

> "Beware of practicing your righteousness before men to be noticed by them; otherwise you have no reward with your Father who is in heaven. So when you give to the poor, do not sound a trumpet before you, as the hypocrites do in the synagogues and in the streets, so that they may be honored by men. Truly I say to you, they have their reward in full. But when you give to the poor, do not let your left hand know what your right hand is doing, so that your giving will be in secret; and your Father who sees what is done in secret will reward you" (Matthew 6:1-4).

How many times do we look for praise from people? It seems like we cannot do anything unless we get recognition from our friends, bosses, or other superiors. We need people to pet our egos and tell us what a good job we are doing; we need atta-boys and other forms of useless praise that, by the way, is our reward in full. That is right — if we seek a pat on the back, that is our full reward. The Bible teaches us that God blesses what is done in secret. If we seek to please God and to do all to His glory, we will not need the praises of men. I do not want to be recognized for the things I do, because I want to work for the audience of One. I want to hear "Well done, my good and faithful servant" from the Lord of Lords and the King of Kings. Pride says "Look at me," while humility says "Look to

Jesus". Pride is what keeps us from forgiving people completely. Complete forgiveness includes reconciliation, no matter what the violation. Maybe we need to get Hollywood to read the Bible since all we see is people getting even with whomever, however and we sit mesmerized because we know in our flesh it is what we all desire. Jesus says; "Truly I say to you, to the extent that you did it to one of these brothers of Mine, even the least of them, you did it to Me" (Matthew 25:40b). The good, the bad, and the ugly. Do not miss this. If we treat people with arrogance, looking down on them because of what they have or have not done, we are treating Him with contempt. If we hate others, then we cannot truly love Him. The way we forgive others is the same way He is going to forgive us.

God tells us to let Him be in charge. He directs us to choose love, holding nothing back but pouring our lives out as living sacrifices, just as Jesus did on the cross for us. This type of love requires denial of self — it is suffering. This love says, "God, I cannot do this without the power of Your Spirit working in and through me." Self-denial is suffering so that God will be glorified. Look at what Jesus did to those who hated Him. He did not die just for those who believe but also for those who do not believe. He died for those who spit on Him, beat Him, slapped Him, slugged Him, and nailed Him to a cross. He died for those who berated and mocked Him. Jesus allowed it all, even though He could have stopped the crucifixion and killed the whole lot of those who tried Him and had Him beaten and sentenced to death, including all the soldiers who took part. When Peter drew his sword and tried to fight those who had come to arrest Jesus, "Jesus said to him, 'Put your sword back into its place; for all those who take up the sword shall perish by the sword. Or do you think that I cannot appeal to My Father and He will at once put at My disposal more than twelve legions of angels? How then will the Scriptures be fulfilled, which say that it must happen this way?'" (Matthew 26:52-54).

Jesus knew He was fulfilling the Scriptures and chose to be obedient to God His Father. He did not need angels to save Him. Jesus was and is and will always be God. He chose to humble Himself, give up His life, and trust His Father. And each one of us is just as guilty for His death on the cross as each one of those who took part in His historical crucifixion. Jesus could have stopped it all — but He chose love for all of us despite the abuse, the cruelty, the hate. What power is greater than love? None! Love "bears all things, believes all things, hopes all things, endures all things. Love never fails" (1 Corinthians 13:7-8a). Jesus proved that by dying for our sins. If we want to please God, we must live according to His desire and not our own, which is the exact opposite of what the world teaches.

Strength Under Control

The world teaches us that saying you're sorry is a sign of weakness, when it takes more courage to admit that we are wrong and seek forgiveness than to act as if we are tough and heartless. Please! Any bully can be cruel and heartless; but the truth is that they are miserable and need to make others miserable in order to feel good about themselves. It is easy to act tough — try being meek. Meekness is great power under control. Try being humble. Jesus chose to be meek and humble and yet has all power and authority. The world tells us to get revenge, which only leaves us empty, bitter, resentful, and full of hate. The world teaches us to do unto others before they do unto us. Again, this takes no great effort — but restraint does, self-control does, discipline does, and so do meekness and humility. It takes far more strength to be meek and humble than to be cruel and hateful. This is the higher calling God has given us — not living by our own power but by His. "'Not by might nor by power, but by My Spirit,' says the Lord" (Zechariah 4:6). Jesus demonstrated meekness by choosing to lay His life down for us. He willingly died so that we could live. The Bible teaches us to follow His example.

When you think about our power, it becomes apparent that our power is quite limited and really quite pathetic. We cannot change people, but we can choose to change ourselves with God's help. We can read God's Word and allow it to change us. The more time we spend reading God's Word, the more it can change us. It makes me really sad that the commandments of God are no longer permitted in the school house and seldom seen in the workplace or places of business. Imagine if we were to be inundated by the commandments of God — if everywhere we went we read "Do not steal, do not kill, do not bear false witness, love God, do not take His name in vain." Do you think it would have an effect on our society? Instead we are inundated by slogans similar to "Alcohol brings great happiness," "The one who has the most toys wins," "Shop until you drop," "What we have to offer is bigger and better," "Practice safe sex," "Abortion is pro-choice," and the list goes on. "If it feels good, do it. Live life to the fullest." The truth is that some of the highest causes of death in the United States are bad diets, lack of exercise, suicide, and abortion. That does not sound like life to the fullest to me.

19

Self-Love

People say that they want to know what God's will is for their lives. In God's Word He tells us what His will is for us. "Rejoice always; pray without ceasing; in everything give thanks; for this is God's will for you in Christ Jesus" (1 Thessalonians 5:16-18). It does not sound all that difficult to live out our lives according to God's will. Being joyful is easy enough, once we understand that God's presence in our lives brings joy in the good times and the bad. Just knowing that He is with us, no matter what we are facing or what our circumstances are, we can have joy because of His presence. Praying continually is easy enough, once we realize that breath prayers are every bit as important as prayers uttered in our quiet place in the stillness. Breath prayers are when we say something like "Help me, Jesus." Maybe I hear someone in the office talking and God tells me to pray for them. Perhaps I am driving down the road when God brings someone to mind. I do not have to stop, bow my head, and close my eyes; I just tell God what is on my heart. I talk with God just as I would talk with a person throughout each day — that is praying continually. God is real — there is nowhere we can go away from the Spirit of God. Nevertheless, giving thanks in every circumstance brings a certain challenge. How do we give thanks when our circumstances are hurtful, even abusive? How can I be thankful when I have lost someone through death, divorce, or estrangement?

I can say from personal experience that I have a hard time giving thanks in all circumstances. I have learned that I can be thankful because I know God was with me and will be with me. Being thankful is a choice. Focusing on God and His greatness will help me rise above a life of pain. God knows me better than I know myself and knows how to be the comfort I need, if I will only allow Him. I have also learned that I need to be thankful for each day I am given, and I am learning not to take anything or anyone for granted. God does not even allow the weather to have control over my joy. I love thunder and lightning, rain and snow; and I find an ice storm to be absolutely beautiful. I do not like it when people are hurt because of storms, but I do not want to complain because God chooses to bring rain to nourish the earth or snow in the winter. I do not want to grumble about anything, since it robs me of thankfulness. It is impossible to give thanks in all circumstances if I have a grumbling and complaining heart. Have you ever noticed how grumbling and complaining can rule our lives? We complain about the weather, our jobs, our children, our friends, our spouses, our parents, our in-laws, our teachers, our bosses, and on and on and on. Soon we are complaining about the clothes we wear, the food we eat, the houses we live in, the cars we drive — and we are miserable.

Being thankful can cure a grumbling and complaining heart. When we grumble and complain, we are telling God that His provision is not good enough. Remember when we were children — each new day was an adventure, and the last thing we worried about was what clothes we had to wear, what car we drove, or where we lived. All we cared about was getting outside, finding others to play with, and looking for adventure. What happened? When did "things" begin to cloud our vision and rule our joy? What about the people that God placed in our lives — when did we begin to think they are worthless and unworthy of our love? When we have become unthankful and unholy, we are railing against the sovereignty of God. We begin to focus on what we do not have instead of being thankful for what God has chosen to give us. We are so in love with self that we choose not to be satisfied by God. Our wants and desires outweigh what the Creator of the universe wants for us. Our love for self begins to eclipse our love for God. Things become more important than God: making money, seeking pleasure, having the best of everything — home, cars, iPod, television screen, audio equipment, furniture, and the list goes on. Our mates do not seem as special as they once were, so we look for someone who will make us feel more special for the moment. The devil is rolling around on the floor, holding his stomach in laughter, saying, "All I have to do to get people confused about who they are and who God is, is to give them things or to take away all their things."

We believe the lie that things can make us happy and different people bring us happiness, and we become infatuated with them. That means we must keep on buying things and finding different people who will infatuate us for the moment. It becomes a never-ending battle to bring happiness; and in the end we are left empty, disillusioned, frustrated, and alone, even when surrounded by people who love us. And how many lives have we destroyed in the process of finding happiness? Only a personal and intimate relationship with the Creator of the universe can truly bring us joy, everlasting joy. Happiness only lasts for a moment. Choosing to love God and to give ourselves away to people is God's perfect plan.

A Sinner Among Sinners

When I begin to believe that I am not as bad as other people, I am judging others to be less than me — I am better, therefore I deserve better. The truth is that we all deserve death. Remember the Scripture that says, "There is none who does good, there is not even one" (Romans 3:12b)? When the rich man comes to Jesus and calls Him good, "Jesus said to him, 'Why do you call Me good? No one is good except God alone'" (Mark 10:18). When Jesus is teaching His disciples and the crowd about giving gifts to our children Jesus says "you . . . being evil". That's right — while teaching His followers and His disciples, he calls them evil. "If you then, being evil, know how to give good gifts to your children, how much more will your Father who is in heaven give what is good to those who ask Him!" (Matthew 7:11). Think about this for a moment. According to God's law, if we hate anyone, we are murderers. If we look upon a man or woman with lust, we have committed adultery. How many times have we dishonored our parents, told lies, coveted what someone else had, or stolen something, no matter how small? How many times have we talked negatively about someone or disrespected someone to their face? How many times have we broken the Sabbath, used God's name in vain, or bowed down to another god? Are we consumed with television, computer games, pornography, sex, or any other thing that keeps us from worship? Well, guess what — we are evil. We are no better than rapists, murderers, and the most vile people who ever lived. God says; "Whoever keeps the whole law and yet stumbles in one point, he has become guilty of all" (James 2:10).

Let's go back to the first and greatest commandment. Is it even possible for you to love the Lord your God with all your heart, soul, mind, and strength? And if so, do you? Love is supposed to be patient and kind, without envy, jealousy, or arrogance. Love is not supposed to keep a record of wrongs. Do you have a list that you point out to those who hurt you? I do. I am trying to lose that list. I like the way the NASB puts it: "Love does not take into account a wrong suffered" (1st Corinthians 13:5c). Have we let go of all the wrongs we have suffered? In the following verse it states that love "bears all things, believes all things, hopes all things, endures all things" (1 Corinthians 13:7). Have we chosen to love? Are we bearing all things? Are we believing all things? Are we hoping all things? Are we enduring all things? Here is the problem with us: our flesh is weak, and we cannot be the people that God has called us to be without His power working in and through us. God tells us that it is "'not by might nor by power, but by My Spirit,' says the Lord" (Zechariah 4:6). I know God is moving each one of us to a place of total dependence on Him. When we need God's help, all we have to do is ask. When we are powerless, God is all powerful. We serve the Almighty God! And He stands near, waiting for us to call on Him for help to live in a way that glorifies Him. God calls us to die to self, to suffer. Jesus told us to pick up our crosses and follow Him. "If anyone wishes to come after Me, he must deny himself, and take up his cross and follow Me" (Matthew 16:24).

The cross of Jesus Christ is not about pretty jewelry but about suffering. It is about being treated wrongly, disrespectfully, hatefully, and choosing to love. The cross is about being used, despised, abused, and tossed aside, yet choosing to forgive and work toward reconciliation. It is not something we can do under our own power. God has to work in us and through us

— walking daily, moment by moment, helping us to love those who have hurt us deeply. God has called each one of us who have named the name of Jesus to be ministers of reconciliation.

> "Therefore if anyone is in Christ, he is a new creature; the old things have passed away; behold, new things have come. Now all these things are from God, who reconciled us to Himself through Christ and gave us the ministry of reconciliation, namely, that God was in Christ reconciling the world to Himself, not counting their trespasses against them, and He has committed to us the word of reconciliation" (2 Corinthians 5:17-19).

"Not counting their trespasses against them" — being a sinner, I love that last statement. God has reconciled us to Himself and does not count our trespasses against us. Are we doing the same? Are we asking God to help us to forgive, to choose love, or does the past control us? If our past controls us, we are being used by Satan. Life is about putting the past behind us and calling upon God's divine power to choose to forgive. But most of us want revenge, or we choose to hate in order to protect ourselves. We cut people from our lives instead of working toward reconciliation. That is what pride does. Help me, Jesus!

20 ———————

Sin

Have you ever wondered just what is meant by the word sin? Sin is anything we have done wrong; and it is not hard to understand, since we know (for the most part) what is right and what is wrong. Stealing is wrong, lying is wrong, cheating is wrong, murder is wrong, talking badly about someone is wrong, et cetera. The things we do wrong usually hurt others as well. Divorce, sexual sin, and adultery hurt families; so do murder, hate, unforgiveness, and on and on. I have never forgotten something that I have heard several times., "Sin will take you further than you ever wanted to go and sin will keep you longer than you ever wanted to stay and sin will cost you more than you ever wanted to pay." We all have sin in our lives, and we also have an adversary who wants us to be imprisoned by sin. If our enemy can keep us living in sin, focusing on our sins or the sins of others, he wins. Sin is when we do the opposite of what God wants us to do, even though we know we will struggle with it all our lives. But when you read the Bible, you will learn that the ultimate sin is unbelief. That is right — the ultimate wrong act is not believing in God. "Take care, brethren, that there not be in any one of you an evil, unbelieving heart that falls away from the living God" (Hebrews 3:12). It is the only sin that will not be forgiven. God has created us to worship Him — even to think there is no God is a great tragedy.

> "Know therefore today, and take it to your heart, that the Lord, He is God in heaven above and on the earth below; there is no other. So you shall keep His statutes and His commandments which I am giving you today, that it may go well with you and with your children after you, and that you may live long on the land which the Lord your God is giving you for all time" (Deuteronomy 4:39-40).

God created the heavens and the earth and God has surrounded us with beauty, intrigued us with so much of His creation, and then revealed Himself to us through His Son Jesus Christ. The reason is simple. God created us, and He loves us more than we can ever comprehend. Put aside anything negative that you believe about God for a moment, and please do not miss this. Think about creation: after God created the heavens, the earth, and everything in them, He got down on the ground and formed Adam from the dust of the earth. Then God did something different to man than to any other of His creations. God "breathed into his nostrils the breath of life; and man became a living soul" (Genesis 2:7). In his book *Once An Arafat Man* (great book, by the way — a must-read), Tass Saada talks about how humbled he was by the picture of God on His knees, forming man from the dirt. Then God came very close to His new creation and breathed life into his nostrils. I wonder what that moment was like, when Adam sat up, and the Creator of the universe was on His knees admiring His new creation with a smile. Think about it: the first person that Adam saw when he took his first breath was God. How awestruck Adam must have been. Can you imagine? Wow! What Adam saw, we all desire to see. Adam walked with God in the Garden. Adam and Eve walked with the creator of the universe, talked with Him, were touched by Him, and, most of all, were loved by Him. How sad Adam and Eve must have been when they were deceived by the enemy and put out of the Garden, out of God's presence — how sad God must have been.

Do You Really Love Him?

Can you imagine how sad God must be because a large majority of His creation does not believe in Him? Many say they believe in God but do not live like He is part of their lives. If I truly believe that God loves me and wants me to love Him more than any other person or thing, then my lifestyle will reflect that love for Him. My life has certain qualities because I have chosen to believe that God is real, that He created me, and that He died on a cross so that I can live. One of those qualities is joy — a joy that will not go away. Even in times of hurt, disappointment, or great suffering, the joy is still there because I know that God is with me. He is helping me, sustaining me, and using these things to draw me closer to Him. That is what tests and trials are supposed to do — draw us closer to Him. During these times we call out to God from brokenness and pain, and He hears us. "The Lord is far from the wicked, but He hears the prayer of the righteous" (Proverbs 15:29). The wicked are those who do not believe in God and trust in themselves; the righteous are those who do believe in the only true God and put their trust in Him.

"The Lord is near to all who call upon Him" (Psalm 145:18a). "'Call to Me and I will answer you, and I will tell you great and mighty things, which you do not know'" (Jeremiah 33:3). In the book of Acts, the apostle Paul says that God "is not far off from each one of us; for in Him we live and move and exist" (Acts 17:27-28). James 4:8 tells us to "draw near to God and He will draw near to [us]." In Matthew 28:20, Jesus tells us that he will be with us always. God is right there, waiting for us to seek Him, waiting for us to reach out to Him in faith. God wants a personal and intimate relationship with each one of us. He wants to walk with us, talk with us, guide us through this life, and lead us safely home. He knows that life is a struggle, and He is standing by to help us find our way. All we have to do is to choose to believe and then act on that belief by seeking Him through His Word and prayer. It takes about as much effort and enthusiasm as anything else we give our affections to, but the benefits are endless and eternal. Think about that the next time you sit down for a few hours of television, video games, or searching the Internet. Choose life, or choose to die slowly, playing or doing something insignificant that brings no real, lasting pleasure.

Does peace rule your life? I have a peace because I know He is with me and that He will never leave me or forsake me (Matthew 28:20). In Acts 23:11 and 2 Timothy 4:17, we see these words concerning Paul in times of great difficulty: "The Lord stood at his side" and "The Lord stood with me." God tells Jeremiah, "'Am I a God who is near,' declares the Lord, 'and not a God far off? Can a man hide himself in hiding places so I do not see him?' declares the Lord. 'Do I not fill the heavens and the earth?' declares the Lord" (Jeremiah 23:23-24). Almighty God, the God of all gods, the Lord of lords, and the King of kings promises to be near to us over and over again. How awesome is that? The God who created the heavens, the earth, the seas, and all that is in them wants to be in a relationship with each one of us. He wants us to believe in Him and to work at getting to know and understand Him. "Thus says the Lord, 'Let not a wise man boast of his wisdom, and let not the mighty man boast of his might, let not a rich man boast of his riches; but let him who boasts boast of this, that he understands and knows Me, that I am the Lord who exercises lovingkindness, justice and righteousness on earth; for I delight in these things,' declares the Lord" (Jeremiah 9:23-24). What an awesome thought: God tells us that we can understand and know Him.

How sad it is to think that there are many who choose not to believe. When I think about those who do not believe in God, and I look at their lives, I can only wonder. Where do you go when your world begins to crumble around you? Who do you turn to in times of deep sadness and pain? Where do you go when all of life's problems overwhelm you? To a bottle or a pill? Do you turn to a psychic, look to the stars, worship the sun, or pull yourself up by your own boot straps? And to think that God is right there, reaching out, begging for you to believe. How must God's heart hurt for the ones who choose not to believe, especially since His ultimate desire is for us to know Him. Read Psalm 139 — this is how God is toward each one of us. King David wrote this psalm, but it is true of us as well. "How precious also are your thoughts to me, O God! How vast is the sum of them! If I should count them, they would outnumber the sand. When I awake, I am still with You" (Psalm 139:17-18). "You have taken account of my wanderings; put my tears in Your bottle. Are they not in Your book?" (Psalm 56:8). God wants us to know that He took time when He created us. "I will give thanks to You, for I am fearfully and wonderfully made; wonderful are Your works, and my soul knows it very well" (Psalm 139:14). Make this psalm personal and you will be encouraged; for it is what God wants you to know about His connection to you.

Remember, the greatest sin we can commit is living a life of unbelief toward God. Unbelief says, "I can do what I please, when I please, no matter who I hurt in the process."

> "But you, beloved, building yourselves up on your most holy faith, praying in the Holy Spirit, keep yourselves in the love of God, waiting anxiously for the mercy of our Lord Jesus Christ to eternal life. And have mercy on some, who are doubting; save others, snatching them out of the fire; and on some have mercy with fear, hating even the garment polluted by the flesh. Now to Him who is able to keep you from stumbling, and to make you stand in the presence of His glory blameless with great joy, to the only God our Savior, through Jesus Christ our Lord, be glory, majesty, dominion and authority, before all time and now and forever. Amen" (Jude 1:20-25).

21

A Vain Thing

Where I grew up, curse words were a common thing, except, of course, for the F-word. I would hear "GD" or "JC" on a regular basis, but not the one word thought to be the most vulgar word that being the F-word. Once I was out on my own, I used to take pride in how many times I could use the F-word in a single sentence. I could make men wince by my coarse talk. It was, however, because of my mother's upbringing that I spared women from such filthy language. You would never know it now, since the worst word I use now is "crap," and that rarely. What bothers me the most is the fact that Christians use God's name in vain far more than I ever hear lost people screaming out "JC" or "GD." I hope it is because we do not realize that when we use "OMG," "Lord," "God," "Jeez," "Lordy," or whatever term we choose, if we are not talking about God or to God we are using His name in vain. That is correct — when we use God's name as an expression of surprise, disgust, anger, or exasperation, we are using God name in vain. Using God's name in vain means we make God's name to be meaningless. "Good Lord" at the start or end of a sentence that has nothing to do with God makes His name meaningless. It is using God's name in vain. The expression "Oh my God" is using the Lord's name in vain. It doesn't matter if you say it, write it, or text it. If I use God's name to emphasize whatever I am trying to say, I am using it as a curse word.

I am not doing God a favor by invoking His name, and it is not something that pleases Him. In fact, it is against what God desires from us. "You shall not take the name of the Lord your God in vain, for the Lord will not leave him unpunished who takes His name in vain" (Exodus 20:7). Did you catch that? God will not let the person go unpunished who uses His name in vain. I wonder how many of our ailments, sicknesses, or diseases are due to our sin? I hear Christians beginning and ending their sentences with some form of God's name, and then sometime during the conversation they tell of their allergies, headaches, migraines, or some other illness they have; and it makes me wonder if perhaps God chooses not to heal. I am not saying that all our ailments are caused by sin; but clearly healing can be withheld if we show no respect for the healer. How can I say I love God and use His name as a curse word? That is what it means to profane the name of our God. I profane God's name when I use His name as a show of surprise, displeasure, anger, or disgust. Using God's name with such great disdain is not living in obedience to God. "He who turns away his ear from listening to the law, even his prayer is an abomination" (Proverbs 28:9). We need to remember this the next time we invoke God's name. Is God choosing not to answer or even listen to our prayers when we choose to profane His name? That is what this verse says.

It is, after all, the third commandment that we are breaking when we profane God's name, when we take the name of God in vain. "He who has My commandments and keeps them is the one who loves Me; and he who loves Me will be loved by My Father, and I will love him and will disclose Myself to him" (John 14:21). What does this say about our relationship with God? Can I really say I love God and yet not keep the commandments that He has given — commandments that were given in order to bless my life with good things like healing, strength to make it through each day, heaven, eternal life, or the greatest gift given, God's presence and power? How many blessings am I missing because of my sin? "Behold, you have sinned against the Lord, and be sure your sin will find you out" (Numbers 32:23b). God knows us better than we know ourselves and loves us anyway. God loves us with an unconditional love greater than any love we have ever experienced. He wants to be involved in our daily lives. The point that I am trying to make here is that it is really quite simple to stop using God's name in vain. How much better off will I be with this one simple act of obedience? God blesses obedience. I want God to not only hear my prayers but also to answer my prayers in a way that truly blesses me and those around me. It is my desire to do and say things that are pleasing to God. My life is hard enough without inviting disaster into my life by choosing to use God's name as a curse word.

God Help Me Be Obedient

What would happen if God's people decided to stop doing things that are against God and His Word? What if God's people decided to start doing things we are not doing, in order to be the Christians God has called us to be? I believe God is hurt by His people because of our wants and desires for things that do not satisfy. I believe He is hurt by those of us who say we believe in Him and yet do not give Him the time of day. We would rather watch TV, play on a computer, or read a book than spend time alone with God in contemplation of His Word. There are a host of things that demand our time. We do them because they need to be done or because they bring us pleasure. But how many of them include God? I can do my work in a way that glorifies God. I can do chores around the house in a way that glorifies God. I can even play in a way that glorifies God. But if I do not have a time set aside for reading and contemplating God's Word, I have no real relationship with Him.

Prayer is a great and wonderful way to spend time alone with God, but it is me telling God about my needs or the needs of others. Spending time alone with God by reading His Word is how we hear Him talking to us. He uses His Word to increase our faith, to teach us truths that can change the way we act or believe, to soften our hearts and make us stronger Christians who can help a hurting world. It is really unbelievable just how powerful God's Word is and how He will use it to make us holy and blameless. We will still struggle with sin and will never be perfect until that day we stand before His throne in heaven. However, by spending time alone with God in a two way conversation, listening to His voice as we read the Scriptures, we will become vessels ready for the Master's use. We will be able to beat back depression, anxiety, and all kinds of diseases that plague us. We will be set free from false beliefs. But the greatest thing about spending time alone with God is that we will come to know Him! Every time we read God's Word, we are saying, "God, I love you and I want to know you more."

How many people think that just because they say they believe they will be able to spend eternity with God? Without faith it is impossible to please God. Faith comes by believing and trusting, by choosing to believe and confessing that God is your savior because Jesus died for your sins and God raised

Him from the dead. Remember Romans 10:9-10? You must also know that "faith" in the Scriptures is an action word. You must act on what you believe. Otherwise when you stand before the judgment seat of Christ and you say, "God, I told people that I believed in You; I was a good person and I helped others; I went to church," and so on, God will say, "Go away, for I never knew you." Why would God make us spend an eternity with Him in heaven if we never wanted to spend any time with Him on earth? It is even more terrible for those who truly do know the Lord and yet spend all their time avoiding time alone with Him. We say, "God, I love you, but I do not have time for you today. Bless me anyway." Each day it is the same: God waits patiently for us to spend time with Him, our Creator, the One who gives us life and breath, the One who is near to us every moment of every day. God calls to us and says, "Come near to me; spend time alone with me so I can strengthen you and be real to you. I want to bless you with My presence. I want to whisper encouraging things into your ears. I want to sing over you, My child." But we say, "Not today, God," and another day goes by filled with possessions and chores and games we play — and we wonder why our lives feel empty, unfulfilled, and without purpose.

> "Therefore I urge you, brethren, by the mercies of God, to present your bodies a living and holy sacrifice, acceptable to God, which is your spiritual service of worship. And do not be conformed to this world, but be transformed by the renewing of your mind, so that you may prove what the will of God is, that which is good and acceptable and perfect" (Romans 12:1-2).

If you have not spent time alone with God, I have a challenge for you. Pray and ask God to help you, to show you the time He has set aside to be with you. Then, when you feel God prompting you, stop immediately, go get your Bible, and find a quiet place without distractions to enjoy being taught by the Most High God. What great and mighty things God has prepared to teach you! Are you up to the challenge? God is pleased with this type of obedience because it says, "God, I cannot do this on my own power. Each day I seem to choose not to do this; but if you will help me, then I know it will come to pass."

I will finish with this. Often I pray and ask God to help me to love Him with all my heart, soul, mind, and strength, because I know this is how God wants me to love Him. I also ask God to help me to worship Him in spirit and in truth, because I know this is how God wants to be worshipped. I know these two truths because I have read them many times in His Word. Do you think God is going to answer this prayer? You had better believe it — this is the kind of prayer God wants to answer. So let's get started!

> "Now faith is the assurance of things hoped for, the conviction of things not seen. For by it the men of old gained approval. By faith we understand that the worlds were prepared by the word of God, so that what is seen was not made out of things which are visible. By faith Abel offered to God a better sacrifice than Cain, through which he obtained the testimony that he was righteous, God testifying about his gifts, and through faith, though he is dead, he still speaks. By faith Enoch was taken up so that he would not see death; and he was not found because God took him up; for he obtained the witness that before his being taken up he was pleasing to God. And without faith it is impossible to please Him, for he who comes to God must believe that He is and the He is a rewarder of

those who seek Him. By faith Noah, being warned by God about things not yet seen, in reverence prepared an ark for the salvation of his household, by which he condemned the world, and became an heir of the righteousness which is according to faith. By faith Abraham, when he was called, obeyed by going out to a place which he was to receive for an inheritance; and he went out, not knowing where he was going. By faith He lived as an alien in the land of promise, as in a foreign land, dwelling in tents with Isaac and Jacob, fellow heirs of the same promise; for he was looking for the city which has foundations, whose architect and builder is God. By faith even Sarah herself received ability to conceive, even beyond the proper time of life, since she considered Him faithful who had promised. Therefore there was born even of one man, and him as good as dead at that, as many descendants as the stars of heaven in number, and innumerable as the sand which is by the seashore.

All these died in faith, without receiving the promises, but having seen them and having welcomed them from a distance, and having confessed that they were strangers and exiles on the earth. For those who say such things make it clear that they are seeking a country of their own. And indeed if they had been thinking of that country from which they went out, they would have had opportunity to return. But as it is, they desire a better country, that is, a heavenly one. Therefore God is not ashamed to be called their God; for He has prepared a city for them.

By faith Abraham, when he was tested, offered up Isaac, and he who had received the promises was offering up his only begotten son; it was he to whom it was said, "In Isaac your descendants shall be called." He considered that God is able to raise people even from the dead, from which he also received him back as a type. By faith Isaac blessed Jacob and Esau, even regarding things to come. By faith Jacob, as he was dying, blessed each of the sons of Joseph, and worshiped, leaning on the top of his staff. By faith Joseph, when he was dying, made mention of the exodus of the sons of Israel, and gave orders concerning his bones. By faith Moses, when he was born, was hidden for three months by his parents, because they saw he was a beautiful child; and they were not afraid of the king's edict. By faith Moses, when he had grown up, refused to be called the son of Pharaoh's daughter, choosing rather to endure ill treatment with the people of God than to enjoy the passing pleasures of sin, considering the reproach of Christ greater riches than the treasures of Egypt; for he was looking to the reward. By faith he left Egypt, not fearing the wrath of the king; for he endured, as seeing Him who is unseen. By faith he kept the Passover and the sprinkling of the blood, so that he who destroyed the firstborn would not touch them. By faith they passed through the Red Sea as though they were passing through dry land; and the Egyptians, when they attempted it, were drowned. By faith the walls of Jericho fell down after they had been encircled for seven days. By faith Rahab the harlot did not perish along with those who were disobedient, after she had welcomed the spies in peace. And what more shall I say? For time will fail me if I tell of Gideon, Barak, Samson, Jephthah, of David and Samuel and the prophets, who by faith conquered kingdoms, performed acts of righteousness, obtained promises, shut the mouths of lions, quenched the power of fire, escaped the edge of the sword, from weakness were made strong, became mighty in war, put foreign armies to flight. Women received back their dead by resurrection; and others were tortured, not accepting their release, so that they might obtain a better resurrection; and others experienced mocking and scourging, yes, also chains and imprisonment. They were stoned, they were sawn in two, they were tempted, they were put to death with the sword; they went about in sheepskins, in goatskins, being destitute, afflicted, ill-treated (men of whom the world was not worthy, wandering in deserts and mountains and caves and in holes in the ground. And all these, having gained approval through their faith, did not receive what was promised, because God had provided something better for us, so that apart from us they would not be made perfect. Therefore, since we have so great a cloud of witnesses surrounding us, let us also lay aside every encumbrance and the sin which so easily entangles us, and let us run with endurance the race that is set before us, fixing our eyes on Jesus, the author and perfecter of faith, who for the joy set before Him endured the cross, despising the shame, and has sat down at the right hand of the throne of God" (Hebrews 11:1-12:2).